Ever wanted to benefit from Japanese people paying rent for their apartments?

Or from businesses paying for offices in prestigious districts of Paris?

Or from tourists buying clothes in the trendy shops of Soho London?

Or from jet setters tanning themselves at Mediterranean luxury resorts?

Or from Australian wine vinyards?

Or even from Bulgarian farmers renting land to grow wheat on?

Or from drinkers having a pint in AB InBev's chain of European pubs?

Or from the warehouses and shipping docks of China?

Now you can!

Ever since so many private real estate companies converted themselves into Real Estate Investment Trusts and held IPOs in the mid-1990s, U.S. investors have been discovering the high dividend yields possible through investing in commercial real estate through publicly owned companies.

REITs do not have to pay taxes on the income they distribute to unit holders—and the government requires them to distribute at least 90%!

This means they pay out a lot more money than ordinary corporations (who have to pay corporate taxes).

REITs are cash cows.

And because, in general, rents get raised for inflation, REIT incomes—and their distributions— go up as the value of our money goes down.

But this is no longer a secret. REITs have been included in the S&P 500 for over ten years, and are now so respectable even old companies and widely known brand names such as Weyerheuser are converting over to REIT status.

What's not so well known is countries all over the world have been following the lead of the United States and creating their own versions of Real Estate Investment Trusts, to help their own commercial real estate sectors and to provide housing for their citizens.

Nearly 40 countries from Australia to Turkey have laws enabling some form of REITs, using the US as a model but ringing their own changes.

By investing in foreign REITs you can:

1. Have a stream of income that's not dependent on the US dollar (or euro, or yen, or whatever your currency of residence is).

2. Have a stream of income from economic activity that may be up while your local area is down.

3. Worldwide inflation protection

REITs
Around the World

Your Guide to Real Estate Investment Trusts in Nearly 40 Countries for Inflation Protection, Currency Hedging, Risk Management and Diversification

Richard Stooker

ISBN-13: 978-1466437012

ISBN-10: 1466437014

LEGAL NOTICE

DISCLAIMER

I am not a broker. I am not a licensed securities dealer or representative of any kind.

I am no legal right to sell you securities and I'm not trying to do so. Nothing in this book is to be construed as a solicitation or offer to sell you securities. Nothing in this book is to be construed as personal financial advice.

I have no legal right to give you personal financial advice. Even if I were a registered financial advisor, I don't know you or your individual financial situation.

This book is the result of my research and is believed accurate. It consists of my opinions and suggestions.

I'm not making any representations as to how much money you will make if you invest according to the guidelines I set forth—that will depend upon the payouts of dividends and interest of the precise securities you decide to invest in, and nobody can predict the future.

That is part of the problem with mainstream financial advice—it assumes the future will repeat the past. It doesn't. Past performance is not indicative of future results.

This book is for education and entertainment.

Nothing in this book is to be construed as professional advice. For that, you should consult your attorney, accountant or financial adviser. I am not responsible for the results of your investment decisions.

I follow my own advice. The only financial investments I own, besides ordinary checking, savings and money market accounts, in my IRAs and my taxable brokerage account, are ones I recommend in this book.

I am not seeking to raise the price of those securities by making them more popular. I will not sell them unless driven by financial emergency. You must read, think over what I say, make your own investment decisions and take responsibility for your own life, including the results of your investment decisions.

Continuing to read this book implies your acceptance of these terms.

Table of Contents

Introduction

"Ninety percent of all millionaires become so through owning real estate." - Andrew Carnegie

Like to travel?

Like to stay and shop in nice places?

Like to make money from your investments?

This book is intended to help you do all three.

"REIT" stands for Real Estate Investment Trust and is a particular form of real estate company which is allowed by law to not pay taxes on the money it distributes to its owners—and it's required to pay out at least 90%.

This is nearly ideal for income investors. People who bought them up, especially in the middle 1990s when there was a boom in REIT Initial Public Offers (IPO), have made out like bandits.

Today in the US, REITs have become respectable. Not quite stodgy, but even in this bear market their yields are not as high as they were back when only a select few knew about and understood the opportunity they represented.

The new frontier is now REITs outside the United States. Some of them are also established and respectable (Canada and Australia), but other markets are still a wild and wooly frontier.

REITs are great for people who believe the above quote by Andrew Carnegie (and similar ones attributed to other famous people), but are unwilling or unable to invest directly in real estate.

If you buy a second house to rent out, or other properties, you can make a lot of money, but you need:

1. Time to look around for the properties and to do everything else required

2. Negotiating skills

3. Repair and renovation skills (or dependable contractors to do the work for you at an affordable price)

4. Cash and a good credit record

5. Skills to find and keep good tenants

6. To be available, or arrange to have a backup, in case your tenants have problems

7. Enough ongoing cash to keep up with repairs

The risks:

1. Bad tenants can trash your property before the law allows you to evict them (and I've heard of them sneaking back into properties)

2. Your local market can go down in value (and quality of the neighborhood)

3. Destruction of the property (of course you better have insurance, but it's still a hassle at best)

4. You're tied down to the locality

5. If you aren't qualified to be a landlord, or don't want the hassles, you can hire a management company to do the work for you and just send you a check for your net profit every month, but they can be notoriously unreliable. In St Louis years ago, two brothers running a real estate management company ran away to Chile to escape the law. One of them eventually went to jail. The other jumped off a roof. The land owners they stole from didn't get their money back.

6. If you want to sell, it can take months to get your money. In the current economy it can take years.

Unless you're really turned on by being a landlord (some people are), it just makes a lot more sense to tell your broker to buy Real Estate Investment Trust units just as though they were shares of stock.

REITs Around the World

The success of REITs in the United States did not go unnoticed around the world. It took a few years, but eventually other companies began to pass similar laws.

Nearly 40 countries now have them, or at least have passed the laws. (In a few countries the law has been passed but is being held up by the taxing authority. In a few others, the law is there but no real estate entrepreneurs have formed one, or converted their existing real estate companies to the REIT form.).

Why You Should Invest in REITs in Other Countries

REIT investors should diversify:

1. Geographically

Just as local real estate markets can rise and sink independently of each other, the 2008 financial crisis taught us that can happen to entire countries. The US real estate market was devastated, and many countries in Europe were hit hard. But Canada wasn't affected much at all. Australia also looks to have a great future.

2. Capital flows

US REITs mainly invest in the US, because the country is big enough to hold plenty of opportunity without the risk of leaving it.

But as I touched on in Chapter 37, owning property/REITs in other countries allows you to profit from economic transactions taking place far away in another country or continent.

3. Currencies

The value of the US dollar has been sliding downhill for decades. Even slight inflation adds up over time.

And its near-term prospects seem bad. To try to prevent a depression in 2008, the US government took on the risk of bad assets from the financial institutions. Plus it's spent a lot of money on various stimulus and buy out schemes.

The US taxpayer is being treated as a bottomless gold mine, but of course we're not. We haven't broken yet, but we're struggling.

The Federal Reserve monetized some of our enormous national debt, directly creating inflation.

And despite all these efforts, the economy has barely budged, and unemployment is the highest it's been for decades.

However, the US dollar looks good compared to the euro which is threatened by the bankruptcy of Greece (and possibly Italy, Spain, Ireland and Portugal) as I write.

The British pound is not getting any press here, but the UK government also owes a heck of a lot of money.

And Japan owes something like twice its Gross Domestic Product, which is double the rate for the US. Despite that, currency traders are buying the yen, driving up its value. However, that's nothing to count on, because the Bank of Japan is selling yen like crazy to keep its value down.

Switzerland has the strongest currency in Europe, but the Swiss government wants to keep the franc's value down because it's an export-driven country and a rise in the franc makes it lose money.

However, the economies and dollars of Canada and Australia are looking good right now.

You could buy Canadian and Australian certificate of deposits, but the purchasing power of that interest income would go down in time thanks to inflation. And interest rates in those two countries are very low, as they are all around the world.

So why not get some Canadian and Australian dollar income flows that will go up with inflation, because they come from dynamic, innovative businesses that can raise rents?

Real Estate Investment Trusts

And why not also get some rental income from some of the most promising currencies of the developing countries—such as Singapore and Hong Kong?

And remember, you don't know the future. Maybe Europe will get itself together, and you'll want a steady stream of euro income from REITs as well.

Whatever happens with Greek government bonds, people in Europe will continue to need apartments to live in and shops to buy food from.

Our Trip Around the World

This book takes you on a tour of those countries. I cover what I can of REITs in each one.

One thing I cannot do is evaluate those countries for their accounting practices and advise you on how to evaluate the REITs.

For one thing, although REITs are trusts in the US and many countries, in many they are other business entities. Accounting practices differ from country to country. I don't pretend to be an international legal and accounting expert.

In some countries the laws aren't being taken much advantage of—yet. It's easy to forget after the law was passed in the US, it was three years before the first REIT was listed on the stock market.

And even then the industry remained immature—little known and confused with fraudulent real estate partnerships—for 30 more years.

The early 1990s gave the industry a big boost because of that period's recession. A lot of high quality commercial properties were foreclosed on and taken possession of by banks.

Who didn't want them - they wanted money.

So the new REITs took the money they'd raised from the stock market and went bargain shopping at the banks.

Many private real estate companies decided it'd be to their financial advantage to switch to REIT status, so investors got the opportunity to own a piece of some of the best real estate portfolios in the country.

Advantages of REITs to Governments

In a lot of countries, property sales are private, and kept secret…that is, not reported to the government so everybody can avoid paying taxes on the transaction.

Therefore, some governments are passing REIT laws hoping to make their local commercial real estate markets more transparent and tax-efficient.

Some countries suffer from extreme shortages of properties such as residential apartments and houses. The government wants to encourage private investment capital to build more apartments and houses for people, so offers tax-free profits as an incentive.

Our Itinerary

I'll start out covering some basic information on REITs and their professional associations around the world.

Then we'll start on our journey. I'll begin with REITs in the United States, because every trip starts where you already are (you may not be a US resident, but I'm from that country).

Then we'll head north to Canada, then south to Mexico, sail out into the Caribbean, and then south to the rest of Latin America.

Then we cross the Atlantic Ocean to the United Kingdom, visit the rest of Europe, and keep moving East to the Gulf Region, down to Africa, and then on to Asia and Australia, then finish up in New Zealand.

Along the way we'll read a few excerpts from our guidebook.

Then we'll finish up with the most important part—how you can profit from investing in REITs.

If you wish to learn more about the individual REITs in each country, you can visit my website:

http://www.incomeinvesthome.com/growth/reit/

There's a page on every REIT I could find substantial information on, and that's almost all of them.

Ready?

First boarding call.

Chapter One

What are Real Estate Investment Trusts

REITs started in the United States as a 1960 law, The Real Estate Investment Trust Act of 1960, part of the Cigar Excise Tax Extension Act of 1960 signed by President Dwight D. Eisenhower. Congress wanted to give small investors a chance to profit from commercial real estate as wealthy individuals and institutions have traditionally done.

The law allows investors to pool their money to acquire ownership interest in real estate properties, without having to own real estate directly—especially commercial real estate.

Until then, individuals had to own real estate directly. However, it could be difficult for them to raise enough money to buy a second house or an apartment building, and even harder for one person to buy an office building or a shopping mall.

Those who did so needed a variety of skills to make the investment profitable, and they were still at risk from business conditions in their local area. Not to mention having to fix toilets at 2 o'clock in the morning.

The REIT structure in the United States is the blueprint. However, as they've spread around the world—especially becoming popular since 2000—individual countries have come up with their own variations.

What makes them especially attractive for income investors is the provision they do not have to pay federal income taxes on the net income they distribute to unit holder—and they're required to pay out at least 90%.

Therefore, they generally pay a lot more money than regular corporations—which are subject to federal income taxes.

In the United States, REITs are trusts, not corporations. Therefore, when you want to invest in them, you buy up units, not shares. You are a unit holder.

U.S. law gives REITs a lot of freedom. They can do almost anything so long as it's related to real estate. They may develop land, build buildings, buy properties, renovate them and sell them.

These are known as equity REITs.

In the United States—and this is rare in the rest of the world—REITs may also enter the business of real estate financing. This is primarily for businesses, but some mortgage REITs were engaging in subprime mortgage lending until the 2007-2008 crash. Since that time, some new mortgage REITs have been started to take advantage of the bailout money being offering by the U.S. government to deal with the "toxic" assets—poor performing mortgages—on the books of many large financial institutions. This may be profitable for awhile because the US Federal Reserve has pledged to keep interest rates low for the next few years.

A few REITs engage in both activities, so they're known as hybrid REITs.

Many countries impose more restrictions on what activities a REIT may engage in. For instance, many—though not all—prohibit REITs from owning property outside that country.

Others have restrictions on development and resale of properties.

In the U.S. and some other countries REITs can be private, which means they're not listed on a stock exchange and available for sale only to Accredited Investors (in the US)—or publicly listed on a stock exchange where you and I can use brokers to buy them on the secondary market.

For the most part, I ignore private REITs except in a few countries where there're no other REITs to write about.

Some countries allow only publicly listed REITs.

Some real estate companies have chosen to be publicly traded companies, or C corporations in the United States, but not to elect the tax status of REITs. These are known as real estate operating companies, or REOCs. Therefore, a REOC is not required to pay any dividends, just like other companies listed on a stock exchange. Therefore, the share price of a real estate operating company is more volatile, because there's no immediate reward for investors.

Many countries impose leverage or gearing restrictions on REITs, though the U.S. does not. That is, they declare a REIT may not borrow more than a certain percentage of the value of a building. This may prevent them from buying a good building, but is intended to keep REITs on a financially sound basis.

REITs Around the World

REITs can be very general, or very specialized.

Some specialize by type of real estate—such as office buildings, self-storage or luxury apartments. Some buy every kind of property from farmland to parking lots.

Some specialize by geography. They'll invest only in Southern California. Some go all over the map.

Because REIT and REIT-like companies—of course many of them have different names in different countries and different languages—operate under varying legal structures, I have not attempted to analyze their accounting rules and conventions.

In the U.S., you analyze equity REITs by looking at things such as their Funds From Operation FFO and Adjusted Funds From Operation AFFO. That does not necessarily apply to REITs in other countries.

Chapter Two

REIT Industry Organizations

Real Estate Investment Trusts are now represented around the world by three professional organizations:

National Association of Real Estate Investment Trusts (NAREIT)

European Public Real Estate Association (EPRA)

Asian Public Real Estate Association (APREA)

National Association of Real Estate Investment Trusts

http://www.nareit.com/

NAREIT is the American trade organization for REITs, and also promotes the interests of similar real estate companies around the world.

Their slogan is: REITs: Building Dividends and Diversification.

Although it's primarily a voice to represent every REIT, you can also join if you are a real estate professional or otherwise interested in the industry. You can join as an associate member instead of a corporate member.

Your membership includes a large number of sources of additional information about the REIT industry:

Online Handbook and membership directory.

NAREIT Slideshow about the basics of Real Estate Investment Trusts and the publicly traded real estate industry.

Federal REIT Tax Compendium—an interactive tool for researching all IRS rulings regarding Real Estate Investment Trusts.

Real Estate Portfolio magazine—all about real estate and investing in REITs.

Half off the regular price of NAREIT conferences.

Complimentary copies of various other industry magazines, including: Financial Standards Updates/Alerts, IRS REIT Guidance, Look Who's Talking About REITs and Publicly Traded Real Estate, Look Who's Talking Around The Globe, NAREIT Domestic Returns, NAREIT Global Daily Return, NAREIT NewsBrief, NAREIT Quick Member Guide and the State and Local Tax Policy Bulletin.

You get a discount on various other publications.

You get access to these research publications: Data Library; (comprehensive source for industry performance statistics and capital market activities), REITWatch; NAREIT's online statistical report; and NAREIT's monthly online publication that summarizes trends in the REIT and publicly traded real estate industry.

The NAREIT Website Contains a Wealth of Information on the REIT Industry

Their subsidiary site http://www.investinreits.com/ contains more information on how to invest in Real Estate Investment Trusts.

They also act to promote investments in REIT stocks in many ways—for instance, by lobbying Congress to pass legislation to add a real estate index option to the federal employees' Thrift Fund.

They also promote high quality, uniform accounting standards for real estate investment trusts to practice. It would immensely benefit REIT investors if they could easily compare Funds From Operations (FFO) and Adjusted Funds From Operations (AFFO) figures across all companies.

They also sponsor the FTSE NAREIT US Real Estate Index Series and the FTSE EPRA/ NAREIT Global Real Estate Index.

The front page of their web site contains links to interesting stories about REITs in the financial press.

European Public Real Estate Association (EPRA)

http://www.epra.com/body.jsp

The European Public Real Estate Association (EPRA) is the trade association of publicly listed real estate companies or Real Estate Investment Trusts (REIT) in Europe.

The EPRA now has over 200 members, including property companies and investors. It was founded in 1999, is a nonprofit organization and is based in Brussels, Belgium. They work to encourage investment is REITs in Europe, and to encourage best practices across the industry.

Asian Public Real Estate Association

http://www.aprea.biz/

The Asian Public Real Estate Association (APREA) is a non-profit industry trade group of Asian Real Estate Investment Trusts. It is based in Singapore. It is for both publicly listed and private Real Estate Investment Trusts, and was established in 2005.

Generally, APREA's goals are to promote real estate investment, promote the interest of REITs and to represent the industry to governments in the region. Jaime Ysmael of Ayala Land Inc is the President. They currently have 134 members, including institutional investors, REITs, other commercial real estate companies, real estate consultants and law firms.

They operate an educational program for real estate professionals, though the APREA Institute.

They have Chapters in Singapore, Australia, Hong Kong, Japan, Korea and India.

Therefore, the Asian Public Real Estate Association is working hard to promote property investment in Asia. They don't cover Real Estate Investment Trusts only, but may encourage countries in Asia which don't currently on REIT laws on their books to create REITs in their countries as well.

Chapter Three

Real Estate Investment Trusts in the United States - REITs

The first one started up in 1963.

Their popularity grew slowly at first. In the 1980s they got confused with real estate partnerships which were tax scams sold to unwary investors by brokers.

However, the 1990-92 recession gave them a big boost.

In those years, a lot of commercial real estate properties had their mortgages foreclosed on by banks. But banks don't like to own such real estate, so they were happy when REITs lined up cash in hand to acquire quality properties for a cheap price.

From 1993-95, lots of private real estate companies chose to go public as a REIT to raise the cash to take advantage of these deals.

And gradually investors learned what a good deal REITs were for them.

REITs did great until the financial crisis of 2008-2009.

Many mortgage REITs, especially the ones who had been active in the subprime mortgage market, went out of business.

Some REITs were de-listed and became private companies.

In 2009 the IRS adjusted the rules to allow REITs to issue new units in lieu of cash distributions.

This happened because the financial crisis was very hard on some REITs. Obviously, getting new units instead of cash quarterly distributions did not go over well with investors who bought REIT units for the income.

However, REITs in general have recovered pretty well from the crisis. While private real estate companies have struggled to obtain the credit they need, REITs were able to get funding from the public capital markets.

Publicly listed REITs in the United States can choose to work directly in the real estate business by developing, buying, renovating, owning and managing and selling property.

These are known as equity REITs.

They may also choose to engage in real estate financing.

Those are known as mortgage REITs.

Essentially, they make money by borrowing money for a cheap interest rate and then loaning it out at a higher interest rate.

This can work well. But in the financial crisis of 2008 many of them got hammered. When the credit markets froze, they could no longer borrow money, but still owed money on their obligations.

Mortgage REITs may do sale/leaseback deals, mezzanine financing and other types of transactions little understood by people outside the business.

In the United States, REITs are set up as legal trusts. They are operated on behalf of the owners—that is, the unit holders.

What makes them especially attractive for income investors is the provision they do not have to pay federal income taxes on the net income they distribute to unit holder—and they're required to pay out at least 90%.

Therefore, they generally pay a lot more money to their unit holders than regular corporations do to their shareholders—which are subject to federal income taxes.

U.S. law gives REITs a lot of freedom to act to build—or lose—unitholder value. They can do almost anything so long as it's related to real estate. They may develop land, build buildings, buy properties, renovate them and sell them.

REITs in the US can be very general, or very specialized. There's one that buys only office buildings in Manhattan. Some own only self-storage facilities, medical buildings, timber land, warehouses or Section 8 apartments.

Some specialize by geography. They'll invest only in Southern California. Some go all over the map.

Because in the U.S. REITs are not corporations, the usual accounting rules and generally accepted principles don't apply.

When you want to evaluate the financial status of most companies, the first figure you want to know is, what is their net operating income? Because if they're not making any money, you don't need to know anything else. Nothing else is important.

But for a REIT, you look first at their Funds From Operations or FFO. That's because REITs own a lot of real estate property, and the law allows them to take depreciation of that property as an expense.

Nothing lasts forever, including the best-constructed buildings, so every year the REIT can write down a percentage of their property because of depreciation.

And this amount is then subtracted from their gross income, to figure their net income.

But the truth is, barring floods, fires and other disasters, modern buildings last longer than depreciation assumes.

And depreciation is a "paper" expense. It's a figure that's deducted from net income, but—unlike other kinds of expenses such as repairs and payroll—it does not take cash out of the company's bank account.

Therefore, it makes more sense when evaluating how well a REIT is handling its cash, to add the depreciation expense back.

And the same thing applies to amortization.

Amortization is much like depreciation, except it doesn't apply to physical objects. It applies to large, one-time expenses. REITs might amortize leasing commissions paid to leasing agents, and tenant improvement allowances, which is the expense of remodeling a property to suit the needs of a particular tenant.

For a lot more details on Real Estate Investment Trusts in the United States, I recommend the book by Ralph Block:

Investing in REITs: Real Estate Investment Trusts by Ralph L. Block

Major REITs in the United States Include:

Kimco Realty:

Kimco Realty (NYSE:KIM) is the U.S.'s largest retail REIT specializing in neighborhood and community shopping centers.

Kimco started in 1960 with a partnership between Milton Cooper, Chairman and CEO, and Martin Kimmel, Chairman Emeritus. Milton Cooper is a well-known and respected leader in the real estate industry.

They operate the kind of small strip shopping that's anchored by a supermarket, a discount department store or a drugstore. Where you go to buy a quick loaf of bread or tube of toothpaste.

Kimco now owns about 2,000 properties in 45 U.S. states, Puerto Rico, Canada, Mexico and Chile.

http://www.kimcorealty.com/

ProLogis Trust:

ProLogis Trust (NYSE:PLD) is the world's largest owner, manager and developer of distribution facilities. They have 542.3 million square feet of industrial space in 132 markets around the world, from North America to to Europe to Asia. Their facilities are located near transportation hubs, such as sea ports, airports, and major highways.

http://www.prologis.com/en/default.aspx

Weingarten Realty:

Weingarten Realty (NYSE:WRI) is has neighborhood and community shopping centers and industrial real estate across the United States, in 23 states. Most of their shopping centers are high class strip malls rather than full-fledged shopping centers.

Weingarten is also one of the oldest REITs in the US.

http://www.weingarten.com/

Simon Property Group:

REITs Around the World

Simon Property Group (NYSE:SPG) is the largest publicly traded REIT in the US. It focuses on regional shopping malls. They're in over 190 locations in the United States—with over 383 properties with 261 million square feet.

It invests in five different types: Premium Outlet Centers, The Mills, community/lifestyle centers, regional malls and international properties in Europe and Asia as well as North America.

http://www.simon.com/

Vornado Realty Trust:

Vornado Realty Trust (NYSE:VNO) is a one of the largest fully-integrated REITs in the United States. They own a diversified portfolio of commercial real estate concentrated in four areas: New York City offices, Washington D.C. offices (Vornado/Charles E. Smith division), retail, and merchandise mart.

http://www.vno.com/index.phtml

Weyerhaeuser Timber:

Weyerhaeuser Timber (NYSE:WY) is a major timber company recently converted to REIT status. This is a "coup" for the industry, because it's a well-recognized brand name. That this company saw value in converting to REIT status helps validate it.

http://www.weyerhaeuser.com/

Other REITs in the US include:

UMH Properties, Inc—United Mobile Homes
http://www.umh.com/

Regency Centers—shopping centers anchored by grocery stores
http://www.regencycenters.com/

Realty Income—single tenant commercial properties
http://www.realtyincome.com/

Public Storage—operating storage space
http://www.publicstorage.com/

Brandywine Realty Trust—office and industrial properties

http://www.brandywinerealty.com/

Brookfield Properties—superior commercial real estate properties
http://www.brookfieldproperties.com/

BRE Properties—residential properties in southern California
http://www.breproperties.com/

Boston Properties—class A office buildings in Boston Massachusetts
http://www.bostonproperties.com/site/index.aspx

Mack-Cali Realty—East Coast USA office and office/flex properties
http://www.mack-cali.com/

Cousins Properties Incorporated—Sunbelt commercial properties
http://www.cousinsproperties.com/

Duke Realty—largest commercial real estate REIT
http://www.dukerealty.com/

Health Care REIT—healthcare industries commercial properties
http://www.hcreit.com/

Highwoods Properties—southern and Midwestern US commercial properties
http://www.highwoods.com/HIWMain/

Hospitality Properties Trust—hotel management
http://www.hptreit.com/

HRPT Properties Trust—office properties
http://www.hrpreit.com/

Kilroy Realty Corporation—high quality commercial property in southern California
http://www.kilroyrealty.com/

Liberty Property Trust—commercial office and flex properties in both the US and UK
http://www.libertyproperty.com/

Lexington Realty Trust—single tenant, net lease commercial properties
http://www.lxp.com/

Maguire Properties—class A office properties in southern California

REITs Around the World

http://www.mpgoffice.com/

National Retail Properties—single tenant commercial properties
http://www.nnnreit.com/

Corporate Office Properties Trust—office properties
http://www.copt.com/

Pennsylvania REIT—retail properties in Pennsylvania
http://www.preit.com/

SL Green Realty Corporation—office buildings in Manhattan New York
http://slgreen.com/

Universal Health Realty Income Trust—healthcare facilities
http://www.uhrit.com/

AMB Property Corporation—leading developer of distribution facilities
http://www.amb.com/

BioMed Realty—specialized real estate for life sciences industry properties
http://www.biomedrealty.com/

Developers Diversified Realty Corporation—shopping centers
http://www.ddr.com/

Digital Realty Trust—IT datacenters REIT focusing in IT needs of companies
http://www.digitalrealtytrust.com/

EastGroup Properties—focused on industrial properties in the U.S. Sunbelt states
http://www.eastgroup.net/

Equity One REIT—neighborhood and community shopping centers in the south
http://www.equityone.net/home/home.cfm

First Potomac Realty Trust—owning industrial and flex properties
http://www.first-potomac.com/

First Industrial Realty—international distribution centers for supply chain
http://www.firstindustrial.com/

Federal Realty Investment Trust—retail property development, redevelopment and

management REIT
http://www.federalrealty.com/

Gladstone Commercial—leasing business real estate and making mortgage property loans to small businesses
http://www.gladstonecommercial.com/

Inland Real Estate Corporation—retail shopping centers in the Upper U.S. Midwest states
http://www.inlandrealestate.com/home.aspx

Monmouth Real Estate Investment Corporation—net leasing commercial industrial properties to long term tenants
http://www.mreic.com/

Mission West Properties—research and development properties in Silicon Valley California
http://www.missionwest.com/

New Plan Excel Realty Trust—retail neighborhood and community shopping center REIT
http://www.nprt.com/home/default.asp

Prime Group Realty Trust—Prime Group commercial real estate in and around Chicago Illinois
http://www.pgrt.com/

Parkway Properties—office real estate property in southern United States and Chicago
http://www.pky.com/

PS Business Parks—leasing office, industrial and flex space
http://www.psbusinessparks.com/

Tanger Factory Outlet Centers—leading manager and owner of factory outlet centers saving consumers money on brand name products
http://www.tangeroutlet.com/

Agree Realty—development and ownership of retail shopping centers, single tenant or grocery anchored
http://www.agreerealty.com/

AIMCO—Apartment Investment and Management Company, largest owner and operator of apartment complexes
http://www.aimco.com/
Acadia Realty—many shopping centers in the Northeast, Midwest and Mid-Atlantic

REITs Around the World

http://www.acadiarealty.com/

AmREIT REIT—they invest in "irreplaceable corner," high quality commercial retail properties in major markets
http://www.amreit.com/fw/main/Home-893.html

Archstone-Smith—luxury apartment communities in major metropolitan areas
http://www.archstoneapartments.com/

Avalon Bay Communities—real estate investment trust owning and operating luxury apartment communities in high barrier to entry, major metropolitan areas
http://www.avalonbay.com/

Saul Centers—neighborhood and community shopping centers, and office properties
http://www.saulcenters.com/

CLB & Associates Properties—regional malls and community centers, retail shopping
http://cblproperties.com/cbl.nsf/index

Cedar Shopping Centers—owns and operates shopping centers anchored by supermarkets
http://www.cedarshoppingcenters.com/default.php

Equity Residential REIT—"America's Choice for Apartment Living" is their slogan
http://www.equityapartments.com/default.aspx

Feldman Mall Properties—invests in enclosed retail shopping malls
http://www.feldmanmall.com/

General Growth Properties—large enclosed shopping malls REIT
http://www.ggp.com/default.aspx

Glimcher Realty Trust—regional, super regional and community shopping malls real estate investment trust
http://www.glimcher.com/

Getty Realty Corp REIT—service stations, convenience stores and petroleum distribution centers
http://www.gettyrealty.com/

Kite Realty Group—quality neighborhood and community shopping centers
http://www.kiterealty.com/

Macerich Company—REIT that invests in major retail shopping centers in growing markets
http://www.macerich.com/home.asp

Ramco-Gershenson Properties—buys and manages shopping centers REIT
http://www.ramco-gershenson.com/

Taubman Centers—high quality regional malls in the U.S., and being developed in Macao China and South Korea
http://www.taubman.com/

Urstadt Biddle Properties—community retail shopping centers in the Northeast United States
http://www.ubproperties.com/

American Campus Communities—real estate investment trust providing high quality housing for the college student market
http://www.studenthousing.com/

Associated Estates Realty Corporation—apartments for affluent markets
http://www.aecrealty.com/

AMLI Residential Properties REIT—provides high quality, expensive apartments for temporary corporate needs
http://www.amli.com/

American Land Lease—manufactured home communities (MHC) for retirees, many age-restricted
http://www.americanlandlease.com/

Colonial Properties Trust—owns many commercial real estate properties in the United States Sunbelt area—the southern states
http://www.colonialprop.com/

Camden Property Trust—one of the largest multi-unit apartment building real estate investment trusts in the United States
http://www.camdenliving.com/internet/html/home.htm

Education Realty Trust—real estate investment trust providing housing for college students
http://www.edrtrust.com/

Equity Lifestyle Properties—high quality resort properties REIT
http://www.mhchomes.com/DBMHC/MHCMain.nsf/vwPages/HomePageMainWDSRIR-4PLPAM

REITs Around the World

Essex Property Trust—REIT that acquires, develops, redevelops and manages multifamily apartment communities
http://www.essexproperties.com/

Gables Residential—REIT slogan—Taking Care of the Way People Live and Forever Great
http://www.gables.com/

Home Properties—owning and operating over 38,000 apartments
http://www.homeproperties.com/

Investors Real Estate Trust—focused on commercial real estate properties in the Upper Midwest of the United States, plus Texas
http://www.iret.com/

Host Hotels & Resorts—largest provider of brand name, luxury and upscale hotels, especially the Marriott brand name
http://www.hosthotels.com/home.asp

Mid-America Apartment Communities—creating apartment buildings with slogan Creating Great Places to Call Home
http://www.maac.net/

One Liberty Properties—REIT that owns and operates commercial properties with long term leases
http://www.1liberty.com/

Post Properties—providing upscale multifamily apartment units
http://www.postproperties.com/

Sun Communities—real estate investment trust for manufactured home communities and recreational vehicle parks
http://www.suncommunities.com/corporate/

UDR, Inc—REIT providing high quality apartment buildings
http://www.udrt.com/

Washington Real Estate Investment Trust—REIT providing commercial real estate properties in the greater Washington DC metropolitan area including Maryland and Northern Virginia
http://www.writ.com/

Ashford Hospitality—REIT providing financing for other companies in the hospitality industry, and making its own direct investments as well http://www.ahtreit.com/

Strategic Hotels & Resorts—upscale hotels for tourists, businesses and conventions, and resorts
http://www.strategichotels.com/

Equity Inns, Inc—largest REIT in the United States for upscale hotels, and other hospitality real estate properties
http://www.equityinns.com/

Extra Space Storage—second largest self storage company in the United States
http://www.extraspace.com/5/index.html

Felcor Lodging Trust—largest owner of upscale, all-suite hotels in the United States
http://www.felcor.com/

Health Care Property Investors—medical properties for the healthcare field
http://www.hcpi.com/

Healthcare Realty—concentrates on medical real estate for providing outpatient services
http://www.healthcarerealty.com/

Hersha Hospitality—institutional grade and upgrade hotels
http://www.hersha.com/

Innkeepers USA Trust—upscale and extended stay hotels in over twenty states and the District of Columbia
http://www.innkeepersusa.com/

LaSalle Hotel Properties—resorts, conventional hotels and luxury hotels
http://www.lasallehotels.com/

LTC Properties—long term care sector of health care industry
http://www.ltcproperties.com/

MHI Hospitality—renovating and upbranding underperforming hotels, making them make profitable again
http://www.mhihospitality.com/

National Health Investors—purchases and leasebacks of health care facilities, and providing mortgage loans to health care providers
http://www.nhinvestors.com/

REITs Around the World

Nationwide Health Properties—senior housing, long term care facilities, medical office buildings
http://www.nhp-reit.com/

Omega Healthcare Investors—invests and provides capital for long term healthcare industry
http://www.omegahealthcare.com/

Sunstone Hotel Investors—45 upscale hotels with great brand names
http://www.sunstonehotels.com/

Senior Housing Properties—senior living facilities, continuing care communities, nursing homes and wellness centers
http://www.snhreit.com/

Sovran Self Storage—Uncle Bob's Self Storage company
http://www.unclebobs.com/company/

Ventas Real Estate Investment Trust—triple net leasing and Master pooled leasing for the health care industry
http://www.ventasreit.com/

U-Store-It—some climate control units at their 400 locations in the United States
http://www.ustoreit.com/

Alexander's Real Estate Investment Trust—REIT that owns 7 properties in New York City area
http://www.alx-inc.com/

Affordable Residential Communities—REIT that is largest owners of trailer parks
http://www.aboutarc.com/

Berkshire Income Realty—acquires, develops, owns and manages multifamily apartment building communities
http://www.berkshireincomerealty.com/

Capital Automotive—provides sale/leaseback financing to automobile dealerships
http://www.capitalautomotive.com/company/company_facts.htm

Crescent Real Estate Equities—resorts and office buildings
http://www.crescent.com/home/home.asp

Dupont Fabros Technology—wholesale data centers

http://www.dft.com/

Eagle Hospitality Properties Trust—upscale, full-service hotels real estate investment trust
http://www.eaglehospitality.com/

Entertainment Properties Trust—REIT that concentrates on charter schools, megacomplex movie theaters and ski resorts
http://www.eprkc.com/

Forest City Enterprises, Inc—office buildings, retail centers and apartment buildings
http://www.forestcity.net/

Franklin Street Properties—commercial real estate REIT
http://www.franklinstreetproperties.com/

HMG/Courtland Properties—resorts, marinas and commercial real estate in Coconut Grove Florida
http://www.hoovers.com/hmg/courtland-properties,-inc./—ID__12000—/free-co-factsheet.xhtml

Medical Properties Trust—concentrated on medical related real estate
http://www.medicalpropertiestrust.com/

National Health Realty—renovating and upbranding underperforming hotels, making them make profitable again
http://www.nationalhealthrealty.com/

Pacific Office Properties Trust—office buildings in the Western parts of the United States including Hawaii
http://www.pacificofficeproperties.com/

Plum Creek Timber—a large timber company
http://www.plumcreek.com/

Presidential Realty—joint ventures for retail centers

Pittsburgh & West Virginia Railroad—railroad branch lines
http://investing.businessweek.com/research/stocks/snapshot/snapshot.asp?capId=297145

Roberts Realty Investors—Georgia commercial real estate and apartment buildings properties

Rayonier—for timber, timber products and resorts on timber land

REITs Around the World

http://www.rayonier.com/

Inland American Winston Hotels—brand name hotels
http://www.inlandamericanwinston.com/

Feldman Mall Properties, Inc—7 enclosed shopping malls
http://www.feldmanmall.com/

First Real Estate Investment Trust of New Jersey—develops commercial real estate in New Jersey, New York and Maryland

Maxus Realty Trust—multifamily apartment buildings REIT

Supertel Hospitality—for limited access, brand name hotels - 125
http://www.supertelinc.com/

Thomas Properties Group—office buildings, apartment buildings and retail outlets
http://www.tpgre.com/

Alexandria Real Estate Equities—properties designed for the life science industries—offices and laboratories
http://www.labspace.com/

DCT Industrial REIT—distribution of bulky goods and industrial properties
http://www.dctindustrial.com/home

Chesapeake Lodging Trust—upper scale hotels in prime market areas
http://www.chesapeakelodgingtrust.com/

Government Properties Income Trust—rents out office buildings to government agencies almost exclusively
http://govreit.com/

Potlatch Corporation—owns timberland in three states
http://www.potlatchcorp.com/

Pebblebrook Hotel Trust—looking for bargains in high quality hotels
http://www.pebblebrookhotels.com/

Terreno Realty Corporation—industrial real estate
http://terreno.com/

Chatham Lodging Trust—upper scale extended stay hotels
http://www.chathamlodgingtrust.com/

Excel Trust—supermarket anchored neighborhood shopping centers
http://www.exceltrust.com/

Piedmont Office Realty Trust—Class A office buildings in top US markets
http://www.piedmontreit.com/cms/content/view/123/65" title="piedmont office realty

Hudson Pacific Properties—office buildings and entertainment related properties in California
http://www.hudsonpacificproperties.com/

Douglas Emmett, Inc—office buildings and apartments in Southern California and Hawaii
http://douglasemmett.com/

American Assets Trust—retail properties in California
http://www.americanassets.com/

CoreSite Realty—has large numbers of server farms
http://www.coresite.com/

Cogdell Spencer—medical properties and health care facilities
http://www.cogdell.com/

CommonWealth REIT—diversified portfolio
http://www.cwhreit.com/about/company.aspx

DiamondRock Hospitality—high class hotels
http://www.diamondrockhospitality.com/

Monmouth Real Estate Investment Trust—net leased industrial properties
http://www.mreic.com/

Sabra Health Care REIT—wide variety of healthcare facilities
http://www.sabrahealth.com/

Stag Industrial—industrial properties
http://www.stagindustrial.com/index.php

Mortgage REITs in the US:

Anworth Mortgage Asset Corporation—invests in the spread between their cost of capital and

interest rate mortgage holders must pay
http://www.anworth.com/phoenix.zhtml?c=66253&p=irol-index

Bimini Capital Management—invests only in securities guaranteed by Freddie Mac, Fannie Mae and Ginnie Mae
http://phx.corporate-ir.net/phoenix.zhtml?c=177499&p=irol-irhome

BRT Realty Trust—lending to companies that don't qualify for conventional loans
http://www.brtrealty.com/

CapitalSource, Inc—large number of debt products for middle markets
http://www.capitalsource.com/

ECC Capital Corporation—subprime mortgages
http://www.ecccapital.com/

Impac Mortgage Holdings—real estate and asset management solutions - consulting
http://www.impaccompanies.com/

MFA Mortgage Investments—hybrid and adjustable rate mortgage backed securities
http://www.mfa-reit.com/

Newcastle Investment—large portfolio of residential, commercial real estate and corporate debt
http://www.newcastleinv.com/

Annaly Capital Management—manages assets and debts
http://www.annaly.com/

PMC Commercial Trust—conventional real estate loans and Small Business Administration (SBA) loans to small businesses
http://www.pmctrust.com/

Redwood Trust—credit-enhancing and securitizing loans
http://www.redwoodtrust.com/

Spirit Finance Corporation—sale/leaseback financing strategies to small businesses
http://www.spiritfinance.com/

iStar Financial—finances real estate projects
http://www.istarfinancial.com/

Thornburg Mortgage—jumbo and super-jumbo ARMs for sophisticated borrowers and investors
https://www.thornburgmortgage.com/mortgage/loans/index.jsp

Arbor Realty Trust—wide range of real estate backed financing and securities
http://www.arborrealtytrust.com/

American Capital Agency—Freddie Mac, Ginnie Mae and Fannie Mae backed securities
http://www.agnc.com/

Anthracite Capital—high yield commercial real estate investments
http://www1.blackrock.com/Default.aspx?cmty=ant

American Mortgage Acceptance—financing for commercial real estate owners and developers
http://www.americanmortgageco.com/

Capital Alliance Income Trust—nonconforming home loans first and second, mainly in California
http://www.hoovers.com/capital-alliance-income-trust/—ID__58455—/free-co-factsheet.xhtml

Chimera Investment—mortgage backed and other asset backed securities
http://www.chimerareit.com/

Capstead Mortgage—invests in real estate related assets
http://www.capstead.com/

Capital Trust—investment real estate and financing management company
http://www.capitaltrust.com/index2.html

Dynex Capital—financial services real estate investment trust
http://www.dynexcapital.com/

Winthrop Realty—acquiring equity and debt securities backed by real estate
http://www.winthropreit.com/default.html

Gramercy Capital—New York City based finance company for commercial real estate
http://www.gramercycapitalcorp.com/

Hanover Capital Mortgage Holdings—subordinated mortgage backed securities but, they claim, none that are subprime
http://www.hanovercapitalholdings.com/

REITs Around the World

Hatteras Financial—adjustable and hybrid adjustable rate mortgage backed securities
http://www.hatfin.com/

CapLease—single tenant commercial real estate
http://www.caplease.com/index.php

Northstar Realty Finance—originating and acquiring real estate related debt
http://www.nrfc.com/

Origen Financial—loans using manufactured homes (trailers) as collateral
http://www.origenfinancial.com/

RAIT Financial—commercial real estate financing to owners and operators
http://www.raitft.com/home.asp

W. P. Carey—commercial real estate holdings financed in 14 countries
http://www.wpcarey.com/

Starwood Property Trust—taking advantage of opportunities created by financial crisis
http://www.starwoodpropertytrust.com/

Apollo Commercial Real Estate Finance—looking for bargains in commercial real estate financing
http://www.apolloreit.com/

Colony Financial—has already bought debt from FDIC
http://www.colonyfinancial.com/

CreXus Investment Corporation—all types of commercial real estate financing opportunities
http://www.crexusinvestment.com/site/default.aspx

Cypress Sharpridge Investments—investing in Agency Residential Mortgage Backed Securities for interest rate spread profits
http://www.cypresssharpridge.com/

Invesco Mortgage Capital—uses government programs to buy cheap mortgage securities
http://www.invescomortgagecapital.com/

PennyMac Mortgage Investment Trust—investing in distressed home mortgages
http://phx.corporate-ir.net/phoenix.zhtml?c=230474&p=irol-corpProfile

American Residential Mortgage—residential mortgages - direct and backing securities http://www.apolloresidentialmortgage.com/

Resource Capital REIT—many kinds of real estate related financing
http://www.resourcecapitalcorp.com/

Chapter Four

Real Estate Investment Trusts in Canada

Canada picked up on the idea of REITs from the U.S., and their REITs are mutual fund trusts akin to other Canadian income trusts. And owning and managing real estate is their main source of income. Unlike US REITs, they don't much engage in the development of real estate.

The first REIT listed on a Canadian stock exchange was Canadian Real Estate Trust, which began on the Toronto Stock Exchange in September 1993.

Canadian real estate trusts are flow through entities (FTEs). The trust pays no taxes as long as they pay out at least 90% of net profits to the unitholders. They then are responsible for paying their individual taxes to Canada's equivalent of the IRS—the Canada Revenue Authority (CRA).

This is through the Canadian Income Tax Act.

Unlike with corporations, therefore, there is no double taxation of net revenue. This should be quite an attractive situation to investors.

Since one form of real estate expense is depreciation, some of the money sent to unit holders is considered return of capital. Return of capital is not taxed, because it's return of capital, NOT income.

(That's because depreciation is not a cash expense. It's just assumed that a given building is worth 10% less than it was last year because of wear and tear. It increases net income, and therefore increases the amount of dividends payable to the trust's unitholders.)

In Canada, this form of depreciation is known as Capital Cost Allowance (CCA).

However, it lowers the unit holder's cost basis in the unit. That means they'll pay higher taxes if they ever sell it.

Moral—don't ever sell your units in Canadian REITs. You don't want to pay a penny more to either the CRA or IRS.

On October 31, 2006 the Canadian government announced—just after an election in which it promised to keep Canadian trust funds tax free—that beginning in 2011 Canadian trust funds would be taxable.

This is known as the SIFT (Specified Investment Flow-Through) legislation.

However, this does not apply to Canadian Real Estate Investment Trusts, so they remain tax-free in 2011 and beyond.

Canadian REITs fall into these categories—

Diversified

Hotel

Mortgage

Retirement

Industrial

Office

Residential

Retail

Canadian REITS Include:

Allied Properties—Class 1 office buildings
http://www.alliedpropertiesreit.com/

Artis REIT—concentrates on commercial real estate that's in Western Canada
http://www.artisreit.com/

BTB REIT—focuses only on property east of Ottawa in Canada
http://www.btbreit.com/

REITs Around the World

Boardwalk—residential apartment buildings
http://www.bwalk.com/

Calloway—shopping centers anchored by a Wal-Mart
http://www.callowayreit.com/Home-Page/

Canadian Apartment Properties—multi-unit apartment buildings
http://www.capreit.net/

Canadian REIT—oldest real estate investment trust in Canada
http://www.creit.ca/

Chartwell Seniors Housing—long term care facilities for senior citizens
http://www.chartwellreit.ca/

Cominar—largest landlord in Quebec and Ottawa
http://www.cominar.com/ENGLISH/accueil_EN.php

Crombie—largest landlord in Eastern Canada
http://www.crombiereit.com/en/topic.aspx?PID=4

Dundee—largest owner of retail, office and industrial properties
http://www.dundeereit.com/

Extendicare—nursing homes in the United States and Canada
http://www.extendicarecanada.com/index.aspx

H&R REIT—commercial properties in Canada
http://www.hr-reit.com/

Holloway Lodging—hotels under various brands
http://www.hlreit.com/en/home/default.aspx

Huntingdon—variety of commercial properties around Canada
http://www.hreit.ca/

InnVest—owns Canada's largest portfolio of hotels
http://www.innvestreit.com/

InterRent—many apartment buildings in Southern Ontario
http://www.interrentreit.com/

Lakeview—chain of hotels in Canada
http://www.lakeviewreit.com/

Lanesborough—retail, office and industrial properties
http://www.lreit.com/

Morguard—Canada's largest integrated REIT of commercial properties
http://www.morguardreit.com/reit.cfm

Northern—apartment buildings in Northern Canada
http://www.npreit.com/

Primaris—mid-market and dominant shopping centers
http://www.primarisreit.com/

Public Storage Canadian Properties—owns many of Public Storage facilities in Canada
http://pscinvestor.com/company-profile

Retrocom—owns mid-level commercial real estate properties
http://www.rmmreit.com/

RioCan—largest owner of commercial real estate trust in Canada
https://riocan.com/homepage.cfm

Royal Host—owns hotels and resorts across Canada
http://www.royalhost.com/

Scott's REIT—leading operator and owner of small box retail properties
http://www.scottsreit.com/

Temple Real Estate Investment Trust—acquiring and managing hotels across Canada
http://www.treit.ca/index.asp

Whiterock—mid-market commercial retail, office and industrial properties in select locations across Canada
http://www.whiterockreit.ca/index.html

Firm Capital Mortgage—Canada's only financing real estate investment trust
http://www.firmcapital.com/cgi-bin/fc/fcc.pl?p=fcmit&r=1

CANMARC REIT—owns many different kinds of property all around Canada

REITs Around the World

http://www.canmarcreit.com/

Leisureworld Senior Care—many long term care facilities for the elderly in Ontario
http://leisureworld.ca/

Northwest Healthcare Properties—many healthcare facilities throughout Canada
http://www.nwhp.ca/Home/main.aspx

TransGlobe Apartment—owns a large number of apartment buildings in urban areas of Canada
http://www.gotransglobe.com/

Chapter Five

Real Estate Investment Trusts In Mexico

Fideicomisos de Infraestructura y Bienes Raices - FIBRA

Mexican legislators amended the Mexican Income Tax Law (MITL)—articles 223 and 224—to allow Real Estate Investment Trusts in Mexico under the term FIBRA (Spanish acronym—Fideicomisos de Infraestructura y Bienes Raices) in 2003, but implementation was delayed because of the tax consequences.

Mexican FIBRAs must be incorporated as real property trusts. They must have a trustee that is a financial institution domiciled in Mexico and authorized to act as trustee. Trusts are governed by the Mexican Law of Negotiable Instruments and Credit Operations.

Mexican FIBRA Legal Requirements

Mexican FIBRAs are similar to REITs in the United States, but there are differences. There is no minimum number of shareholders, and no restriction on how many shares any given individual can own. The Fibra's assets must consist of at least 70% real estate or related to real estate. The other 30% must be invested in Federal Government Securities registered in the National Securities Registry or in bond or money market mutual funds.

FIBRAs must distribute at least 95% of taxable income to shareholders no later than March 15 of the following year.

REITs in Mexico must hold their property for at least four years after date of construction completion or their acquisition of it.

FIBRAs can also be private offerings, as well as publicly listed and traded. Publicly listed FIBRAs must have at least 20% of shares owned by the general public and traded on the secondary market. These are Certificados Bursatiles Fiduciarios (CBFIs).

In 2010 the Finance Ministry helped clear the legal obstacles.

The first Real Estate Investment Trust in Mexico was listed on The Mexican Stock Exchange (BOLSAA.MX) March 2011.

Fibra UNO (FUNO11.MX)
http://fibrauno.mx/

It sold about $300 million in shares—one third to foreign investors, two-thirds to local investors, including large pension funds. It plans to hold sixteen properties in Mexico. Some of the owners of the properties agreed to swap their real estate for shares of stock.

Hopefully Fibra UNO will soon be followed by a "secundo" and many others.

Chapter Six

Real Estate Investment Trusts in Jamaica

I could not find any general information on REIT laws in Jamaica. However, they do have one:

Kingston Properties
http://www.kingstonpropertiesreit.com/

It's based in Kingston. Although it's small, it has a wholly owned subsidiary, Carlton Savannah REIT (St. Lucia) Limited, incorporated in St. Lucia. Fayval Williams is the Executive Director.

It began April 21, 2008 as Carlton Savannah REIT (Jamaica) Limited. It was listed on the stock exchange August 5, 2008. The name was changed to the current one October 8, 2009.

Kingston Properties owns 83 Hagley Park Road and 19 units in the Loft II building at 133 NE 2nd Avenue, Miami, Florida.

It's small, but owns two high class properties.

Chapter Seven

Real Estate Investment Trusts in Puerto Rico

The law authorizing Real Estate Investment Trusts in Puerto Rico—P.R. Internal Revenue Code as amended 1994. PRIRC 1500 to 1502 and 1101(18)—was enacted in 1972 and amended in 2000 and 2006.

I assume Puerto Rico was relatively early in this regard because it's connected to the United States, where the REIT law was passed in 1960.

Real Estate Investment Trusts in Puerto Rico Legal Requirements

They must have at least fifty shareholders or partners. At least fifty percent of the total value of outstanding shares must be owned by more than five people. They cannot be a financial institution or a life insurance company subject to taxation under Subchapter G of the PR IRC.

95% or more of their gross income must come from dividends; interest; rents from real property; gain from the sale of real property; and payments received for executing loans guaranteed with mortgages on real property, or acquire or lease real property.

75% or more of gross income must come from rents from real property located in Puerto Rico; interest on obligations secured by mortgaged on real property or rights to real property located in Puerto Rico; gain from the sale of real property; dividends from stock in another REIT; amounts received for entering into agreements to make loans secured by mortgages on real property, and to buy or lease real property in Puerto Rico.

At least 75% of the total assets is represented by real estate assets, cash or equivalents, and securities and obligations of Puerto Rico.

At least 90% of their income must be distributed to shareholders annually. The REIT before emendation in 2006 was very restrictive, so not many REITs were formed.

Being a Real Estate Investment Trust in Puerto Rico is a Tax Matter

REIT status is primarily about the taxes, so qualifying depends on a company declaring its status. They can be corporations, partnerships, trusts or associations. The Commissioner of Financial Institutions regulates Real Estate Investment Trusts in Puerto Rico.

REITs in Puerto Rico may be listed or private. According to one source, the first listed REIT began in 2008. However, the only names I could find were of private REITs.

Chapter Eight

Real Estate Investment Trusts in Brazil

Fundo de Investimento Imobiliario - FII

In 1993 Brazil launched its version of Real Estate Investment Trusts (REIT), with what are known as Fundo de Investimento Imobiliario, or FII.

This was from Federal Law 8668/93 and instruction 205/94. Now it is by Rulings 472/08 from Comisao de Valores Mobiliarios/Brazilian Securities Commission (CVM). And regulated by the Rules for Fund Operation, where they're registered, then submitted for approval by the Comissão de Valores Mobiliários/Brazilian Securities Commission (CVM).

FIIs can be listed on the stock market, the Bovespa (Sao Paulo Stock Exchange), and must have at least 50 investors. Since 2006, they have been tax free for individuals, but not for companies—provided those persons own less than 10% of the FII.

At least 95% of operating income, and at least 95% of capital gains, must be distributed to unit holders on a semi-annual basis, at the end of June and December of every year.

This income must be from the operation of real estate—rent and capital gains. Income from fixed income investments is subject to taxes and tax withholding of distributions. The use of leverage is forbidden.

These Brazilian REITs can own and operate property investments. However, there are more private ones than publicly listed ones. It is most often used as a special-purpose entity, and funded by private capital. Existing entities cannot be transformed into a FII.

FIIs must be approved by the CVM, and so must subscriptions for units. They must be formed and managed by financial institutions authorized by the CVM.

There is no required minimum capital. An FII is not a legal entity, but a contractual arrangement between investors and a fund manager. They are closed-end, and can have either a limited or indefinite duration.

Most FIIs are small. They own just one, or a portion of one, property. So most Brazilian REITs own one office building or one shopping center or, in one case, one hotel.

A construction company may not hold more than 25% interest in a FII. Unit holders may be legal entities or individuals in Brazil or outside Brazil. There is no discrimination between Brazilian and foreign investors.

A FII is classified as an investment condominium. They are forbidden by law to use leverage, so all their positions are 100% equity. Another limitation is under Brazilian law rental contracts may be re-negotiated only annually, and rents raised only by the amount of the general price increase in the economy.

The CVM website lists 133 FIIs. However, I crosschecked against them with the Sao Paulo Stock Exchange website listed companies, and none of them were listed as being publicly traded. However, other sources say that FIIs are publicly listed there.

Here is the CVM list of Fundos de Investimento Imobiliarios:

1. Aquilla Fundo de Investimento Imobiliario

2. BB FII Progressivo

3. BB Renda Corporativa Fundo de Investimento Imobiliario - FII

4. BC Fundo de Fundos de Investimento Imobiliario - FII

5. BTG Pactual FII - FII Desenvovlvimento II

6. BTG Pactual Fundo de Investimento Imobiliario - FII Recebiveis Imobiliarios

7. BTG Pactual Fundo de Investimento Imobiliario - FII Renda II

8. CSHG Brasil Shopping - Fundo de Investimento Imobiliario - FII

9. CSHG Desenvolvimento de Shoppings Populares - Fundo de Investimento Imobiliario -

REITs Around the World

FII

10. CSHG JHSF Prime Offices - Fundo de Investimento Imobiliario FII

11. CSHG Logistica - Fundo de Investimento Imobiliario - FII

12. CSHG Real Estate - Fundo de Investimento Imobiliario - FII

13. CSHG Recebiveis Imobiliarios BC - Fundo de Investimento Imobiliario - FII

14. Dovel FII

15. Exitus FII - FII

16. FII Brasilio Machado

17. FII Portaleza

18. FII Sigma

19. Fator Verita Fundo de Investimento Imobiliario

20. FII - Presidente Vargas

21. FII Ancar IC

22. FII Anhanguera Educacional

23. FII Araucarias

24. FII BB Votorantim JHSF Cidade Jardim Continental Tower

25. FII BCO BBM Barra First Class

26. FII BM Asset

27. FII Brazilian Capital Real Estate Fund

28. FII Caixa Cedae

29. FII Caixa Desenvolvimento Imobiliario

30. FII Centro Textil Internacional

31. FII Comercial Progressivo

32. FII Comercial Progressivo II

33. FII Comprev

34. FII Continental Square Faria Lima

35. FII CR2 Laranjeiras

36. FII CR2 RJZ II

37. FII Daycoval Renda Itaplan

38. FII ED Almirante Barroso

39. FII Edificio Castelo

40. FII Edificio OurInvest

41. FII Europar

42. FII Excellence

43. FII Fashion Mall

44. FII FCM

45. FII Fidelidade

46. FII Geo Guarapes

47. FII Grand Plaza Shopping

48. FII GWI Condominios Logisticos

49. FII Hermes

50. FII Hospital da Crianca

51. FII Hotel Maxinvest

52. FII Inca II

53. FII Manhattan

54. FII Max Retail

55. FII Memorial Office

56. FII Mercantil do Brasil

57. FII Mistral

58. FII Nossa Senhora de Lourdes

59. FII Nova Morada

60. FII Onix

61. FII Panamby

62. FII Parque Dom Pedro Shopping Center

63. FII Paeo Moinhos de Vento

64. FII Patrimonial II

65. FII Patrimonial IV

66. FII Peninsula

67. FII Phorbis

68. FII Premier Realty

69. FII Prime Portfolio

70. FII Proj Agua Branca

71. FII Property

72. FII Property Invest

73. FII RB Logistica

74. FII Rio Bravo Renda Corporativa

75. FII Rodobens

76. FII Rubi

77. FII Sao Fernando

78. FII Shopping Guararapes

79. FII Shopping Parque d Pedro

80. FII Shopping Patio Higienopolis

81. FII Shopping West Plaza

82. FII Superquadra 311 Norte

83. FII The One

84. FII Torre Almirante

85. FII Toree Norte

86. FII Tropical

87. FII Vereda

88. FII Via Parque Shopping

89. FII Ville de France

90. FII Votorantim Securities

91. Floripa Shopping - FII

92. FP FII Andromeda

93. WM RB Ccapital Fundo de Investimento Imobiliario - FII

94. Fundo de Investimento Imobiliario - FII Campus Faria Lima

95. Fundo de Investimento Imobiliario - FII Top Center

96. Fundo de Investimento Imobiliario BM Cenesp - FII

97. Fundo de Investimento Imobiliario Bussola

98. Fundo de Investimento Imobiliario Caixa Incorporacao

99. Fundo de Investimento Imobiliario da Regiao do Porto

100. Fundo de Investimento Imobiliario Diamante - FII

101. Fundo de Investimento Imobiliario Eldorado – FII

102. Fundo de Investimento Imobiliario Porto Maravilha

103. Fundo de Investimento Imobiliario Votorantim Securities FII

104. Guanabara FII

105. JPP FII - FII

106. JS Real Estate Multigestao - FII

107. Kinea Renda Imobiliaria - FII

108. Lagra FII

109. Loginvest FII Industrial

110. Mais Shopping Largo 13 Fundo de Investimento Imobiliario - FII

111. MSL 13 - Fundo de Investimento Imobiliario – FII

112. Opportunity FII

113. RB Capital Agre - Fundo de Investimento Imobiliario - FII

114. RB Capital Anhanguera FII

115. RB Capital Desenvolvimento Residencial II Fundo de Investimento Imobiliario - FII

116. RB Capital General Shopping Sulacap FII

117. RB Capital Patrimonial V - FII

118. RB Capital Prime Realty I - FII

119. RB Capital Renda I FII

120. RB Capital Renda II Fundo de Investimento Imobiliario - FII

121. Real Minas FII

122. REP 1 CCS - FII

123. Rio Bravo Cibrasec Fundo de Investimento Imobiliario

124. Sabia Fundo de Investimento Imobiliario - FII

125. Salus Fundo de Investimento Imobiliario - FII

126. SCP FII

127. StarX FII - FII

128. TAG GR IV - Fundo de Investimento Imobiliario - FII

129. Tag Oar - Fundo de Investimento Imobiliario – FII

130. TP Corporate - Fundo de Investimento Imobiliario - FII

131. TRX Realty Logistica Renda I Fundo de Investimento Imobiliario - FII

132. VenturaII-A FI Imobiliario FII

Chapter Nine

Real Estate Investment Trusts in Chile

Fondo de Inversion Inmobiliario - FII

Real Estate Investment Trusts in Chile come from Law No. 18,815 on Investment Funds published in the Official Gazette on July 29, 1989 as amended and by administrative regulations contained in Decree No. 864 published on February 23, 1990. They are known under the Spanish name Fondos de Inversion Inmobiliario (Real Estate Investment Fund) or FII.

Legal Requirements of Real Estate Investment Trusts in Chile

A Chilean FII may be public or private. They are unincorporated entities. When public, it must be managed by a corporation, sociedad anonima, registered in Chile. The Chilean Securities Commission - Superintencia de Valores y Seguros - SVS - must approve the FII rules.

There is no legal requirement as to initial capital, but they're supposed to have at least an amount of the equivalent of about three hundred fifty thousand US dollars within a year of formation.

Private Fondos de Inversion Inmobiliario in Chile must have under fifty shareholders. Listed FIIs must have at least fifty shareholders within six months, or at least one institutional investor.

A FII cannot hold investments in another FII managed by the same entity. Liabilities may not exceed fifty percent of assets.

They are not subject to either income or capital gains taxes.

Richard Stooker

Initially they were allowed to invest only in urban real estate located in Chile, marketable mortgage notes, and a specially regulated type of real estate corporation. In 1994 an amendment allowed them to invest in other types of real estate corporations, which can invest in real estate outside Chile.

A FII cannot own shares in another FII which is managed by the same entity. Their debt is limited to 50% of assets

There is no provision under Chilean law for a real estate company to convert to REIT status.

Low Profit Distribution Hallmark of Chile Fondos de Inversion Inmobiliario - FII

At least 30% of the FII in Chile's income must be distributed to their shareholders, thirty days after the annual meeting. This is extremely low. The usual amount is the 90% established in the REIT law of the United States. Unless the return of an FII is suspiciously high, I don't see any reason for foreign investors to put their money into a Chilean Fondo de Inversion Inmobiliario. You'd get a highest rate of distribution from REITs in every other country I'm aware of.

A new amendment prohibits them from direct investment in real estate, which seems to go against the whole REIT concept.

However, at this time there seems to be no publicly listed FIIs in Chile.

Chapter Ten

Real Estate Investment Trusts in Peru

Real Estate Investment Trusts in Peru were established by Article 27 of the Investment Trusts and their Administrator Entities Law (Legislative Decree 862).

Apparently there are some Real Estate Investment Trusts in Peru, but so far I have had no luck finding out anything about them.

Chapter Eleven

Real Estate Investment Trusts in Argentina

Fideicomiso Financiero Inmobiliario

The legal form similar to Real Estate Investment Trusts in Argentina—Fideicomiso Financiero Inmobiliario—began in 1995 by law 24,441.

However, not many companies have made use of this law. There's only one so far.

That's IRSA—Inversiones and Representaciones S.A., the biggest real estate investment company in Argentina. It owns a lot of properties, mostly commercial. Some of the biggest malls in Argentina are owned by IRS.

http://www.irsa.com.ar/irsa/index_eni.htm

Its purpose is the acquisition and management of office buildings, luxury hotels, shopping malls, apartment houses, and land reserves.

It has a subsidiary, Alto Palermo SA (APSA). They also own most of Mendoza Plaza Shopping SA, and the Alto Rosario Shopping.

In June 2008, subsidiary Alto Palermo acquired a site in Beruti 3351/3359, between Bulnes and Avenida Coronel Diaz in Palermo, Buenos Aires, near the shopping center "Alto Palermo Shopping."

Therefore, the one REIT Argentina has is quite big and active. It's also listed on the New York Stock Exchange.

Chapter Twelve

Real Estate Investment Trusts in the United Kingdom

The United Kingdom (UK) has had Real Estate Investment Trusts starting January 1, 2007. This is set out in Part 4 of the Finance Act 2006 (as updated by the Finance Act 2007).

New companies can get approved from the start and older companies can convert to UK-REIT status. They must notify HM Revenue & Customs (HMRC) before the beginning of the accounting period, but do not have to change their corporate structure. In fact, UK-REITs have to be corporations. The most basic requirement is the company is in the property rental business. They are allowed to also conduct other businesses, which however are taxable.

They also must distribute at least 90% of exempted rental income to shareholders to avoid owing income taxes. These are known as Property Income Distributions (PID). In the UK these are taxable at the full marginal tax rate. A REIT may also pay normal dividends, at a schedule of its own choosing, within 12 months of the end of each accounting period.

UK-REITs must be solely resident in the UK for tax purposes. They cannot be an open ended investment company. They must be listed on a recognized stock exchange, including the Main Market of the London Stock Exchange, but not AIM.

Also, every REIT in the UK is required to make certain its rental income is at least 125% of the amount of interest paid on debt. Companies changing to this business structure must pay a one-time tax to the government of 2% of their gross assets. And investments in property must constitute more than 75% of a company's assets.

When they develop property, it must be for investment purposes. They must hold it at least three years after completion of the development.

They must have at least three separate buildings, commercial or residential, and their market value cannot exceed 40% of the total.

Their tax exempt profits must be at least 75% of their total profits.

Groups of companies can make up a Group UK-REIT, including some with noncorporate structures. This can be a principle company along with all subsidiaries it owns 75% or more of. (Except not open ended investment companies and insurance companies.)

The main UK-REITs are:

Land Securities Group:

Securities Group (LSE: LAND) is the largest commercial property company and Real Estate Investment Trust in the United Kingdom. They own 26 shopping centres, 20 retail parks, a total of 19.4 million square feet of retail space. They also own a lot of office and hotel property in London. And twenty-nine Ibis and Novotel (brand names owned by Accor) hotels.

http://www.landsecurities.com

British Land:

British Land Company (LSE: BLND) started out in London in 1856 as a way for ordinary people to have the right to vote. After the Reform Act of 1832, people could vote if they owned a "forty-bob freehold." Companies bought up large tracts of land, then sold freehold rights to obtain a rent of 40 shillings (bob), or two pounds per year, to qualify to vote.

On January 1, 2007 BLND became one of the first UK-REITs, and they are now probably the second largest. They own or manage 13.5 billion pounds of retail properties:

Their focus is on prime "Out of Town" (suburban) retail properties (66% of their portfolio) and office buildings in London (32% of their portfolio), and they're expanding into Western Europe.

http://www.britishland.com/

Hammerson:

Hammerson (LSE:HMSO)is another one of the original UK-REITs to convert as of January 1, 2007. They own and manage prime shopping centers, out of town retail parks and office buildings. They are also listed on the Euronext Paris exchange as a SIIC.

They own sixteen shopping malls and sixteen retail parks with a combined total of 1.6 million square meters of retail space. They own six office buildings with 170,000 square meters.

http://www.hammerson.com/

SEGRO:

SEGRO (LSE:SGRO) holds various kinds of business properties in ten European countries: Spain, Italy, Germany, Belgium, Poland, Czech Republic, The Netherlands, Hungary and France. It's a commercial property investment and development company with office buildings, light industrial, logistics, warehouses and data centre properties. They currently own 5.9 square meters of property worth 5.3 billion pounds

http://www.segro.com/segro

UK REITs Include:

Capital Shopping Centres Group—largest owner and operator of prime regional shopping malls in the United Kingdom, and a split off demerger company from old REIT Liberty International.
http://www.capital-shopping-centres.co.uk/

Hansteen Holdings—many industrial properties in the UK, Germany, France, Belgium and The Netherlands.
http://www.hansteen.co.uk/

Great Portland Estates—owns many buildings in Central London
http://www.gpe.co.uk/

Primary Health Properties—owns primary healthcare facilities throughout most of the United Kingdom.
http://www.phpgroup.co.uk/

Workspace Group—office and industrial space in London for small and medium sized businesses.
http://www.workspacegroupplc.co.uk/

Big Yellow—top self-storage brand name in the UK.
http://www.bigyellow.co.uk/

Shaftesbury—invests only in the fashionable areas of the West End of London.
http://www.shaftesbury.co.uk/

Warner Estate Holdings—operates six real estate funds with various types of commercial properties.
http://www.warnerestate.co.uk/

Pineapple Corporation—this is technically a UK-REIT since it's based in the UK for tax purposes and has UK-REIT status. However, it's listed on the Luxembourg Stock Exchange and does not have its own website. Plus, the website of the Luxembourg Stock Exchange has no information it. There's no information available on it.

Derwent London—owns many London commercial buildings, with great emphasis on style and architecture.
http://www.derwentlondon.com/

Mucklow (A & J) Group—diverse commercial property portfolio mainly in The Midlands of the UK.
http://www.mucklow.com/

Town Centre Securities—a large variety of commercial properties, including car parks.
http://www.tcs-plc.co.uk/

London & Stamford— owns a variety of commercial real estate in the UK.
http://www.londonandstamford.com/

Highcroft Investments—small, owns commercial properties in South East England.
http://www.highcroftplc.com/

McKay Securities—owns a variety of commercial real estate in central London and South East England.
http://www.mckaysecurities.plc.uk/

Glenstone Property Group—currently listed on the Channel Islands Stock Exchange.
http://www.glenstoneproperty.co.uk/

Metric Property Investments—retail properties in the UK.
http://www.metricproperty.co.uk/

NewRiver Retail—shopping centers, especially for food stores, in the UK.
http://www.nrr.co.uk/

Local Shopping REIT—owns over 655 local retail properties throughout the United Kingdom. http://www.localshoppingreit.co.uk/

.

Chapter Thirteen

Real Estate Investment Trusts in France

societe d'investissement immobilier cotee—SIIC

French REITs are known as les societes d'investissements immobilier cotees, or SIICs. They became a legal investment vehicle in France with publication of an executive order dated July 12, 2003. The French government wanted to compete with Belgium, Dutch and German funds.

SIIC rules are slightly different than those for U.S. Real Estate Investment Trusts.

French REITs or SIICs Pay Out 85% Not 90%

French SIICs are exempt from taxes so long as they pay out 85% of their recurring income. Unlike the United States REIT law, they are exempt from taxes on the up to 15% of their income that they do not distribute.

They must pay out 50% of their capital gains within two years, but do not pay taxes on the remaining 50% of capital gains.

Therefore, SIIC (REIT) investors don't receive quite as much cash flow. The SIIC cannot have more than 60% of its stock owned by one shareholder or group of shareholders acting in concert.

These French Real Estate Investment Trusts must be listed in France on the Paris Stock Exchange - now Euronext Paris. However, according to recent law a real estate company can be listed on any qualifying stock exchange, so there is no longer any requirement for foreign companies to set up French affiliates.

They cannot be privately owned. And they must have capital of at least 15 million euros.

Also, they may not provide services.

French SIIC qualifying activities are:

1. Purchase or development of a building with intent to lease

2. Participation in corporate subsidiaries engaged in the purchase or development of buildings with intent to leasing them.

Nonqualifying activities are subject to full, ordinary taxes.

Their properties must be in France. They are not subject to any formal gearing requirements that limit their percentage of balance sheet debt.

Effective January 1, 2009 one shareholder cannot own more than 60% of one SIIC.

They must have a free float of at least 15%.

French real estate companies that convert to the SIIC structure have to pay a 16.5% tax on their unrealized capital gains.

Paris is Europe's biggest office building market, providing a lot of opportunities to French REITs.

In fact, owning office buildings, retail properties and residential buildings in and around Paris is the main activities of French REITs.

US REITs in general own ordinary buildings in ordinary cities and towns in every state. Your local supermarket may be in a REIT-owned strip mall.

However, French REITs focus on Paris. Some of them do have properties in other areas of France, but they are in the minority. As a result, as a whole French SIICs are not geographically diversified.

However, it's probably also true if the economy of Paris is down enough to hurt those SIICs, business is probably also bad in the rest of the country.

SIICs must withhold 25% of distributions to foreign shareholders, but many tax treaties reduce this to 15%.

The professional group representing the SSICs or French REITs is Federation des Societes Immobilieres et Foncieres (FSIF). Jean-Paul Dumortier is chairman.

SIICs in France include:

ADT SIIC—owns 3 buildings in Paris
http://www.adtsiic.eu/

Affine—nearly 100 buildings in 3 countries
http://www.affine-group.com/pages/articles/fiche.php?s_code=historique

AffiParis— owns buildings in Paris
http://www.affiparis.fr/pages/articles/fiche.php?s_code=profil&s_menu=13&s_theme=affiparis&l=en

Alliance Développement Capital—owns 5 buildings in France, 3 in Paris
http://www.adcsiic.eu/

Altarea—hotels in France, Italy and Spain
http://www.altarea-cogedim.com/

ANF Immobilier—owns much of historic areas in Lyon and Marseille
http://www.anf-immobilier.com/

Eurosic—green office buildings in Paris
http://www.eurosic.fr/

Fonciere des Logements (FDL)—owns many thousands of houses in France and Germany
http://www.fdlogements.fr/

Fonciere Atland—buys through sale-leasebacks
http://www.fonciere-atland.fr/home.html

Fonciere Inea—owns nearly 100 properties throughout France
http://www.inea-sa.eu/

Fonciere Massena—owns variety of commercial properties in France
http://www.fonciere-massena.com/

Fonciere des Murs—owns hundreds of properties

http://www.foncieredesmurs.fr/

Fonciere Paris France—many office buildings and industrial properties in and around Paris
http://www.sfpif.com/index_eng.php

Frey—new generation retail parks
http://www.frey.fr/

Gecina Group—largest, office and retail
http://www.gecina.fr/fo/index.php?&id=4&L=1

ICADE—diversified portfolio of properties
http://www.icade.fr/en/#

Immobiliere Dassault – high quality buildings in and around Paris
http://www.immobiliere-dassault.com/

Klepierre—many shopping centers in thirteen European countries
http://www.klepierre.com/majic/pageServer/0f060600pn/en/Home.html

Mercialys—shopping centers in France
http://www.mercialys.fr/home.html

Paref Paris Realty Fund—owns lots of property in Paris region
http://www.paref.com/

SIIC de Paris—buildings in Paris and surrounding area
http://siicdeparis.fr/

Silic—office buildings in Paris
http://www.silic.fr/home.html

Societe de la Tour Eiffel—owns many office buildings, warehouses and light industrial parks in France
http://www.societetoureiffel.com/

Societe de Fonciere des Regions—owns a lot of properties situated all over England.
http://www.en.foncieredesregions.fr/

Societe Fonciere Lyonnaise—owns many office buildings in Central Business District of Paris
http://www.fonciere-lyonnaise.com/en

REITs Around the World

Unibail-Rodamco—The largest REIT/SIIC in Europe
http://www.unibail-rodamco.com/unibail-rodamco/do/ChangeLangue

Zublin Immobiliere France—owns eight office buildings.
http://www.zueblin.fr/fr/index.aspx

Acanthe Development Company—office buildings in Paris
http://www.acanthedeveloppement.com/

Argan Fonciere en Immobilier Logistique—custom designs warehouses
http://www.argan.fr/

CeGeREAL—premium office properties
http://www.cegereal.com/en/

Chapter Fourteen

Real Estate Investment Trusts in The Netherlands

Fiscal Investment Institution - Fiscale Beleggingsinstelling – FBI

In 1969, The Netherlands became the first country in Europe to pass its own REIT law.

One European expert on Real Estate Investment Trusts, Piet Eichholtz, Professor of Real Estate and chair of finance department of Maastricht University in The Netherlands, has studied REITs a lot.

According to him, Real Estate Investment Trusts that specialize by property type do better than those that specialize by geography. This is easier for REITs in the United States to do, because this country has many separate regions.

However, European REITs are largely based on their own countries, so Eichholtz advocates laws allowing pan-European Real Estate Investment Trusts.

Rodamco Europe Netherlands-REIT is one of the largest in Europe.

Netherlands Real Estate Investment Trusts are Called Fiscale Beleggingsinstelling or FBI

The Dutch Corporate Income Tax Act of 1969 introduced the Fiscale Beleggingsinstelling (FBI) for closed end Fiscal Investment Institution. They must pay out 100% of their taxable profits, to avoid taxation. They are not allowed to engage in land and property development. Foreign ownership is limited to under 25% by a single non-Dutch national.

A domestic FBI must be a limited company (BV), a public company (NV), or a joint account (FJA). A foreign FBI must be a comparable entity incorporated or formed under the laws of an EU member country. They can be either listed or unlisted.

The Dutch REIT FBI has Restrictions

Some FBIs or Netherlands Real Estate Investment Trusts are unregulated, but all those publicly listed are regulated.

No owner of more than 45% of an FBI's shares can be an entity other than another Fiscale Beleggingsinstelling. No individual person can own more than 25% of a Fiscal Investment Institution.

15% taxes are withheld from dividend distributions to stockholders, including foreign shareholders.

A company can begin as a Dutch REIT effective only as the first day of a year.

Corio N.V.—largest REIT in Europe. It owns shopping malls in The Netherlands, France, Italy, Spain, Turkey and Germany.
http://www.corio-eu.com/

Eurocommercial Properties—shopping centers in four countries
http://www.eurocommercialproperties.com/

Nieuwe Steen Investments—shops and office buildings
http://www.nsi.nl/

Vastned Offices and Industrial—offices and industrial properties
http://www.vastned.nl/Engels/VastNed_Offices_Industrial/Dashboard/index.aspx

Wereldhave—shopping centers and offices in seven countries
http://www.wereldhave.com/home/

Vastned Retail—many retail properties
http://www.vastned.nl/Engels/VastNed_Retail/Dashboard/index.aspx

Chapter Fifteen

Real Estate Investment Trusts in Finland

Finland passed The Finnish Act on Real Estate Investment Funds in 1998 (Kiinteistörahastolaki, 1173/1997) but, so far, no REITs have actually been set up in that country.

In Finland, REITs are required to have 80% of their assets comprised of residential properties. Their activities are limited to building properties for their own use and renting them out. Debt financing cannot exceed 80%.

At 90% of funds must be distributed to shareholders.

And the REIT must be publicly listed. No single shareowner can own more than 10%.

The Government Recently Made Changes to Encourage Real Estate Investment Trusts In Finland

In early 2010 the Finnish government approved some changes in tax benefits to private real estate companies looking to become REITs, the "tax exemption law" (Laki eräiden asuntojen vuokraustoimintaa harjoittavien osakeyhtiöiden verohuojennuksesta, 299/2009). In May 2010 these were approved by the European Commission.

It's hoped now REITs will be formed in Finland, to encourage development of affordable rental housing.

Chapter Sixteen

Real Estate Investment Trusts in Spain

Sociedades Anonimas Cotizadas de Inversion en el Mercado Inmobiliario—SOCIMI

On October 27, 2009 the Spanish government published Spanish Law 11/2009 governing Spanish REITs in the Spanish Official Gazette. It covers the period beginning January 1, 2009.

Spain's government started introducing the Real Estate Investment Trust structure to Spain several years ago as part of a package to help the country's economy.

Real Estate Investment Trusts in Spain - called Sociedades Anonimas Cotizadas de Inversion en el Mercado Inmobiliario (SOCIMIs) - must be listed. They must have at least 85% of their original 15 million euros in urban property.

The SOCIMI must distribute at least 90% of rental income to shareholders; 50% of profits of sale of property; 100% of income received as dividends from other SOCIMIs and REITs.

Spanish unlisted investment funds will be allowed to convert themselves into a Sociedade Anonimas Cotizadas de Inversion en el Mercado Inmobiliario.

All SOCIMIs are regulated by the Comision Nacional del Mercado de Valores (CNMV).

Spanish Sociedades Anonimas Cotizadas de Inversion en el Mercado Inmobiliario - SOCIMIs - Must Actually Pay Some Taxes

In contrast to other REITs around the world, SOCIMIs will be taxed at 18%, but ordinary shareholders will not pay any further tax on the dividends and distributions they receive. If they receive any nonqualifying income, they pay ordinary Spanish corporate income taxes on that.

Spanish REITs must take the legal form of a listed joint stock corporation (Sociedad Anonima). They require a minimum capital of 15 billion euros. There is a minimum free float of 25%.

Their main activity (minimum of 80% of their assets) is to be the development and purchase of urban real estate. This can include residences, office buildings, retail centers, hotels, and parking lots. They're also allowed to invest in other SOCIMIs, foreign REITs and Spanish or foreign qualifying subsidiaries and shares or units of real estate Collective Investment Schemes as governed by Spanish Law 35/2003.

At least 80% of their income must come from these sources.

The maximum amount of leverage allowed is 80%.

They must hold at least three separate properties, and none of those three may make up more than 40% of the total value of the combined assets.

Properties they buy must be rented out for at least three years. Properties they develop must be rented out for at least seven years.

Spain enjoyed a big property boom before the financial crash, so it's hoped by the government and business people setting up Real Estate Investment Trusts in Spain will bring back the good times.

So far, none are actually listed on Spain's stock exchange.

Chapter Seventeen

Real Estate Investment Trusts in Italy

Societa di Investimento Immobiliare Quotate or SIIQ

In July 2007 the Finance Act (Finanziara budget Law 296) took effect in Italy authorizing their version of Real Estate Investment Trusts (REIT)—the Societa di Investimento Immobiliare Quotate or SIIQ.

They are under the supervision of the Bank of Italy and Consob, and governed by Civil and Tax law.

Italian SIIQs Must Distribute 85%

Italian REITs must generate at least 80% of their income from rental properties and distribute at least 85% of their income to shareholders.

So long as they abide by these guidelines, a SIIQ's income from property rentals is exempt from IRES (corporation taxation) and IRAP the regional taxes which are 3.9%.

A SIIQ must be either: a S.p.A. (Societa per Azioni)—which a joint stock company in Italy for tax purposes or a corporation from outside Italy. All SIIQ shares must be traded on a regulated European exchange.

No shareholder may own more than 51% of the voting rights or right to receive profits. 35% of the shares must be owned by shareholders with no more than 1%.

Any nonrental income the Italian real estate investment trust receives (up to 15% is allowable), including capital gains from sale of property, is taxed at the ordinary corporate rate of 27.5%.

A SIIQ Does Pay Capital Gains Taxes

Ordinary real estate companies that wish to convert to SIIQ status must pay 20% tax on unrealized capital gains.

They must have a minimum of 40 million euros in capital, and "SIIQ" must be part of the company name. Distributions are made annually.

Capital gains are taxed the same as any other real estate company.

Shareholders are subject to having 20% withheld from their dividends.

Few Italian Real Estate Investment Trusts

The Italian real estate industry took a long time to react to the SIIQ law. Of course, it's true the timing was not good. 2007 was the beginning of the worldwide real estate/financial crisis, so REIT IPOs and conversions have more difficult than they would have been prior to 2007.

IGD Immobiliare Grande Distribuzione SIIC SpA is the first and, so far, the only SIIQ listed in Italy. It did not convert to this status until April 2008.

IGD Immobiliare Grande Distribuzione SIIC SpA owns shopping centers, supermarkets and hypermarts. It owns 65 properties in Italy and Romania.

http://eng.gruppoigd.it/

A major property company, Beni Stabili, had been expected to convert to SIIQ status but has not yet done so. It just recently met all the requirements, so it may well convert in the near future.

Chapter Eighteen

Real Estate Investment Trusts in Bulgaria

Special Purpose Investment Companies - SPICs

REITs in Bulgaria come from Act on the Special Investment Purpose Companies Promulgated, State Gazette, issue No. 46 dated May 20, 2003, amended, issue No. 109 dated December 16, 2003, effective from January 1, 2004, amended and supplemented, Issue No. 107 dated December 7, 2004, effective from December 7, 2004). The Financial Supervision Commission of Bulgaria controls their activities.

At least 90% of the Fund's net profit should be distributed as dividends. Dividends must be paid within twelve months of the end of the financial period.

Real estate is the only type of business they may conduct. They are restricted to buying property in the country Bulgaria. Their capital must be at least 500,000 Levs.

They are required by law to have various activities completed by a servicing company. This companies analyzes the state of real estate in the company, performs appraisals and other analysis.

It cannot owe more than 20% for the land it buys. And it cannot put more than 10% of assets into the servicing company.

Many of the Bulgarian REITs I could find info on were pretty nondescript. Unlike nowhere else in the world, REITs in Bulgaria are investing in farmland, woods and vacant lots.

On the other hand, they also have a REIT specializing in health spas and resorts. That is new and interesting twist. Many other REITs have hotels, resorts, and entertainment properties.

Health and Wellness is the only I know of catering to people who go to a resort for better health, not just to relax.

Real Estate Investment Trusts in Bulgaria:

1. Advance Terrafund REIT—largest landowner in Bulgaria behind the government
http://karoll.net/en/?section=investirane_v_advance&id=32

2. Agricultural Land Opportunity Fund Mel Invest REIT—acquires agricultural land or other parcels to renovate and lease them.

3. Agro Finance—owns mainly agricultural land.
http://agrofinance.bg/en/home

4. Agroenergy REIT—buys land to renovate and resell.
http://www.agroenergy.bg/

5. Aktiv Properties REIT—has 10 commercial properties around Bulgaria
http://www.aktivproperties.com/en/home

6. Balkan and Sea Properties REIT—lots to hold cars for sale

7. Bulgarian Investment Group REIT

8. Bulland Investments REIT—agricultural properties and some commercial real estate.
http://www.bulland.org/

9. CCB Real Estate Fund REIT (5CK)

10. CEE Properties REIT (5CG)—

11. City Development REIT (CDX)

12. Elarg Agricultural Land Opportunity Fund—agricultural properties
http://www.elarg.bg/home_en

13. Energetics And Energy Savings Fund REIT (6EE)

14. ERG Capital 3 REIT-Sofia (5ER)

15. Exclusive Property REIT - Sofia

16. Expat Beta REIT—commercial, office, vacation and residential properties

17. FairPlay Properties REIT—commercial, office, vacation and residential properties
http://www.fpp.bg/

18. Forucom REIT-Haskovo (6F4)

19. Intercapital Property Development Real Estate Investment Trust—a summer resort and a winter sports resort
http://icpd.bg/

20. Park Inc (4PK)

21. Premier Fund REIT (4PR)

22. Real Estate Investments Fund - Fini REIT (RRH)

23. Prime Property BG—variety of commercial real estate projects
http://primepropertybg.com/

24. Sopharma Buildings REIT-Sofia (4OX)

25. Sopharma Properties REIT (6S6)

26. Status Properties REIT Sofia (6ST)

27. Super Borovets Property Fund (6SB)

28. Tourin Properties REIT-Sofia (TPS)

29. Zenith Properties REIT-Sofia (Z3T)

30. Bulgarian Real Estate Fund 5BU— one of the oldest and largest REITs in Bulgaria
http://brefbg.com/

31. Benchmark Real Estate (6BMA)

32. Health and Wellness REIT (4H8)— building a string of resort spas
http://www.hwreit.eu/en

33. Invest Property REIT (5IP)

34. Quantum Developments REIT PLC (5Q1)

35. Real Estate Investments Fund - Fini REIT (RRH)

36. Serdica Properties REIT (6SR)

37. HypoCapital REIT (6H1)

Chapter Nineteen

Real Estate Investment Trusts in Germany
G-REITs

Germany introduced a law allowing for their equivalent to Real Estate Investment Trusts (G-REIT) effective January 1, 2007.

The REITAG law was not actually passed until March 2007, and The G-REIT Act was enacted June 1, 2007, but the Ministry of Finance made it retroactive to that January 1.

Germany is the largest real estate market in Europe, so the potential is large. About half of that is residential property, and so the other half is commercial real estate.

A G-REIT must be a corporation listed on a recognized stock exchange, and must have an office and management registered in Germany. Dual-resident corporations are not allowed. And neither are privately held corporations.

They must also distribute at least 90% of distributable profits to shareholders. This includes ordinary income and capital gains (calculated according to the Commercial Code which permits only linear depreciation.). The distribution must be made within 13 months after the end of the annual period. This means G-REIT shareholders could wait over a year to receive their dividend checks.

They must abide by a "widely held stock regulation." That is, at least 15% of shares must be held permanently, an 85% free float maintained. No one shareholder can own more than 10%.

They can have only one class of voting shares, and cannot issue preference shares.

Their primary business must be real estate. They must derive at least 75% of their income from real estate, and at least 75% of their assets must be real estate.

And their real estate business must be the acquiring, holding, administering and operation of properties, not trading them. Within a five year period, a maximum of 50% of a REIT's properties can be sold. The entire portfolio can be turned over in ten years. They may not be a real estate dealer. Sale and leaseback arrangements are allowed.

However, the sale of real estate services is not allowed, except through ownership of REIT-service companies which do not have G-REIT status. That can be a maximum of 20% of a G-REIT's income.

They have a gearing restriction. The amount of leverage they can use is 55%. This means they must maintain at least 45% equity in their properties, or loan to value ratio.

A GREIT Cannot Invest In German Residential Properties Built Before 2007

German REITs that meet these requirements are exempt from corporate income and trade taxes, under the REIT-Gesetz law on German real estate stock companies with publicly listed shares.

The dividends they pay out are subject to personal income taxation without applying the half-income assessment method. Starting 2009, their dividends are taxed at flat rate of 25% plus applicable solidarity supplements and church taxes.

The G REIT law excludes German residential property constructed prior to 2007, so these companies will not be active in apartment buildings until they've had time to build some themselves or buy some built after 2006, or foreign residential properties. The German Social Democratic Party did not want tenants facing market driven rental demands.

Real estate companies that convert to the GREIT structure must pay a 20% tax on unrealized capital gains.

The Deutsche Borse set up three separate indexes for G-REITs—the RX REIT All Share Index contains all G-REITs listed on the Prime Standard and the General Standard. The RX Real Estate Index contains up to 30 REITs and real estate companies from the General Standard. The RX REIT Index contains up to 20 of the largest and most liquid REITs from Prime Standard. This means German Real Estate Investment Trusts will be excluded from the main Dax and MDax indices. The German real estate industry does not like this approach.

It's also required by German law that German Real Estate Investment Trusts put their nature in their name. Their company name must include "REIT-Aktiengesellschaft" or "REIT-AG."

The first G-REIT was alstria Office REIT-AG (FSE:AOX), which became a REIT in April 2007.
http://www.alstria.de

In December 2007, Fair Value REIT-AG (FSE:FVI) followed.
http://www.fvreit.de

Since then, the financial crisis has limited the number of other companies taking advantage of this structure.

The third company to become a G-REIT is Hamborner REIT AG, based in Duisburg. It was the first G-REIT to have converted from a long-established, public company. German law makes this process difficult, but it completed the process in January 2010 and officially became a REIT effective February 18, 2010.
http://www.hamborner.de/

Chapter Twenty

Real Estate Investment Trusts in Belgium

Sicafi Immobiliere - Vastgoed BEVAK

On December 4, 1990 Belgium law introduced a form of publicly traded, closed-end real estate companies termed Sicafi Immobiliere, short for "Societe d'Investissement Immobiliere a Capital Fixe publique." (Fixed capital real estate investment trust). In Dutch it's a Vastgoed BEVAK. A Royal Decree date April 10, 1995 enacted the law, effective May 23, 1995.

Sicafis are regulated by the Belgium Commission Bancaire, Financiere et des Assurances—the Banking, Finance and Assurance Commission. They may invest only in real estate (no third party property development.) on a passive basis. Some development is allowed, but they may not sell it in less than five years. They may invest in subsidiaries engaging in qualified (that is, the same passive real estate) activities. They may invest in hotels, but may not manage them.

Sicafi are closed-end funds with corporate structures. They can be either externally or internally managed. They are listed on the Brussels EuroNext exchange.

Sicafi are Subject to Many Requirements

Belgium Sicafi's debt level is limited to 65% of their net asset values—75% of any one building. That's using true market value, not original value minus depreciation.

They're required to value their portfolio of properties at true market value, so they don't count depreciation. They're not allowed to have more than 20% of their assets in any one property group (no longer applies to properties subject to long term commitments of a Member State of the European Economic Area (EEA) or international organizations in which EEA Member

States participate.). Their interest coverage ratio must be 125%.

They're also required to get independent appraisals of their properties on a quarterly basis. They must follow strict rules intended to prevent conflicts of interest. They can be set up as either a limited liability company or a public limited partnership. When they're listed, there are requirements such as a 30% free float.

They're required to distribute at least 80% of their income to avoid paying corporate income taxes, after net debt reduction and excluding capital gains. Unfortunately, distributions are annual, making them impractical to depend on for retirement income.

All Sicafi Immobiliere must be listed

Private real estate companies do not qualify for Sicafi tax status. Their share capital must be a minimum of 1.25 million euros. They are not subject to shareholder restrictions, so shareholders may be residents of Belgium or Luxembourg, or outside those countries.

They also are not restricted in owning property outside Belgium or Luxembourg. However, this may not be practical because of taxes they have to pay in the other country. If a company converts to SICAFI status, they must pay a 16.995% tax on unrealized capital gains.

Belgium Sicafi are still subject to the 39.9% corporate income tax, but only on a notional tax basis. That is, for income with disallowed expenses or abnormal or gratuitous benefits. In effect, their income from rents and dividends is not taxed. (Provided, of course, they distribute at least 80% to owners.)

They are subject to an annual 0.08% on their net asset value.

If you're a resident of Belgium, the Sicafi is required to withhold 15% of your distributions to make sure you pay your income taxes. However, this is not imposed on foreign investors. This requirement is waived for Sicafi that have at least 60% of their net assets invested in residential properties.

Belgium Sicafi:

Cofinimmo—largest real estate investor in Belgium with office buildings, pubs, and medical buildings
http://www.cofinimmo.com/

Aedifica SCA—residential properties in Belgium
http://www.aedifica.be/index.php?id=12

REITs Around the World

Montea SCA—logistics and semi-industrial properties in Belgium and France
http://www.montea.com/index.php?language=en

Befimmo SCA—large office buildings
http://www.befimmo.be/

Intervest Offices & Warehouses—office buildings and logistics properties
http://www.intervest.be/nl/offices/

Leasinvest Real Estate—office buildings, logistics and retail properties
http://www.leasinvest-realestate.com/DesktopDefault.aspx?tabid=1&index=0.0.0

Intervest Retail—many retail properties in Belgium
http://www.intervest.be/en/retail

Retail Estates—retail
http://www.retailestates.be/index.php?id=1&lng=en

Warehouse Estates Belgium—warehouse properties
http://www.w-e-b.be/

WDP (Warehouses De Pauw)—logistics, warehouses in five countries
http://www.wdp.be/

Home Invest Belgium—residential
http://homeinvestbelgium.be/site/index.php?id=1&lng=en

Ascensio—many different properties
http://www.ascencio.be/fr/index.html

Serviceflats Invest—senior residential properties
http://www.sfi.be/index_flash.htm

Chapter Twenty-One

Real Estate Investment Trusts in Turkey

Gayrimenkul Yatirim Ortakligi - GYO

Turkey is a REIT leader, because Real Estate Investment Trusts in Turkey go back to July 22, 1995, with the Capital Markets Law and Communiqué on Principles Regarding Real Estate Investment Companies Serial VI No. 11. They are set up as corporations (joint stock company) listed on the Istanbul Stock Exchange. They are regulated primarily by the Capital Markets Board (CMB).

The REIT in Turkey began trading in 1997. Existing corporations can convert to REIT status. This can be for a limited or unlimited time period.

The beginning capital of a Real Estate Investment Trust in Turkey is decided by the CMB. The full name of the company must contain the words "Real Estate Investment Company." Registered shares must equal at least 25% of issued capital.

A REIT must invest at least 50% of its capital into real estate, rights to real estate and real estate projects. It is to be concerned primarily with portfolio management. A REIT in Turkey may not be involved with construction, and may not be involved with managing any hotel, hospital, shopping center, business center, commercial parks, commercial warehouses, residential sites, supermarkets, and similar types of real estate. This makes me wonder what they are allowed to invest in.

According to one source, it's buildings, land, development projects, real estate backed securities and government instruments. Yet recent REIT announcements mention such items as shopping centers, this is very unclear to me. They apparently can own office buildings. Luxury gated villa communities, as well as apartment building for low and middle class incomes are also mentioned.

They may invest in foreign real estate, but not more than 49% of their assets.

Dividend distribution is made annually, by the end of the fifth month at the end of their fiscal year. Distribution must be at least 20% of distributable profit.

REITs are exempt from corporate income taxes Corporate Tax Law (art. 5-d/4).

REITs in Turkey are required to publish tables of assets with fairly appraised values by certified appraisers. The government's intent here is to bring more transparency to the real estate market in general. Many private transactions are not recorded, to keep valuations low and to avoid paying taxes. But this is inefficient.

There is a Turkish REIT Association.

Real Estate Investment Trusts in Turkey:

EGS Gayrimenkul Yatirim Ortakligi AS (EGYO)

Atakule Gayrimenkul Yatirim Ortakligi—diversified commercial properties
http://www.atakulegyo.com.tr/eng/

Akfen Gayrimenkul Yatirim Ortakligi—hotels in Russia and Turkey
http://www.akfengyo.com.tr/565.aspx

Akmerkez Gayrimenkul Yatirim Ortakligi—owns Akmerkez Shopping Center
http://www.akmgyo.com/

Alarko Real Estate Investment—agricultural properties and others
http://www.alarkoyatirim.com.tr/

Dogus Gayrimenkul Yatirim Ortakligi—owns 2 shopping center and office complexes
http://www.dogusgyo.com/Default.aspx?path=/en

Is Gayrimenkul Yatirim Ortakligi AS—variety of land and commercial properties
http://www.isgyo.com/Default.aspx

Kiler Gayrimenkul Yatirim Ortakligi AS (KLGYO)

Marti Gayrimenkul Yatirim Ortakligi AS)—a hotels and a marina
http://www.martigyo.com/

REITs Around the World

Nurol Gayrimenkul Yatirim Ortakligi AS —a luxury residence in Ankara, Istanbul
http://www.nurolgyo.com.tr/tr

Pera Gayrimenkul Yatirim Ortakligi—a variety of land and projects
http://www.peragyo.com/english/hakkimizda.asp

Sinpas Gayrimenkul Yatirim Ortakligi—major luxury housing and recreation projects
http://www.sinpasgyo.com/en-US/Default.aspx

TSKB Gayrimenkul Yatirim Ortakligi AS—variety of land and properties
http://www.tskbgyo.com/

Vakif Gayrimenkul Yatirim Ortakligi—office buildings and land
http://www.vakifgyo.com.tr/index.asp

Yapi Kredi Koray Gayrimenkul Yatirim Ortakligi—variety of commercial real estate properties
http://www.yapikredikoray.com/en/default.asp

Emlak Konut Gayrimenkul Yatirim Ortakligi—Turkey's largest REIT
http://www.emlakgyo.com.tr/

Saglam Gayrimenkul Yatirim Ortakligi AS—diversified REIT
http://www.saglamgyo.com.tr/en/

Chapter Twenty-Two

Real Estate Investment Trusts in Greece

Real Estate Investment Companies—REICs

In Greece, Real Estate Investment Trusts (REITS) are known as Real Estate Investment Companies (REIC), and the first one was listed June 28, 2005, although the articles 21-31 of law L.2778/1999 authorizing them was passed in December 1999.

The law was flawed at first, so some changes were made by amendments.

REICs must be listed on the Greek Athens Stock Exchange. They are for the exclusive purpose of managing a portfolio of real estate mainly, but can also own securities and cash.

They must own initial capital of at least 29.35 million euros.

Eurobank began in 2003.

Over 80% of the Greek REIC's assets must consist of real estate property in Greece or in the European Economic Area (EEA). This may include subsidiaries which are at least 90% owned and engaged exclusively in real estate activities.

The Greek law defines real estate as commercial business property - this seems to exclude residential and undeveloped land.

They may hold real estate in a non-Greek or non-EEA country, but that cannot be more than 10% of their total portfolio. REICs can invest in moveable assets to meet operational needs, but this is limited to 10% of their total.

One individual property investment may not exceed 25% of the REIC's total asset values.

A REIC is Required to Emphasize Ownership and Management, Not Speculation

They cannot develop property from the beginning. They may own property under development only if it's within 25% of the final cost.

Greek REICs may not invest more than 25% of their net worth in property bought through financial leasing arrangements. And each such contract may not exceed 10% of their total net equity.

And no more than 10% of their properties can be ones in which they hold less than 100% ownership.

They're also forbidden from flipping properties. Once they buy a property, they cannot sell it for at least 12 months.

Leverage, or gearing, is restricted to 50% of the value of their portfolio.

Greek Real Estate Investment Trust Requested Minimum Distributions are Low, but Tax-Free

These Greek Real Estate Investment Trusts must distribute at least 35% of their annual net profits.

Greek REITs do not pay income taxes, but must pay an annual 0.2% tax on their asset values. But their property taxes are only 0.1% instead of 0.6%, and when they buy property, they're exempt from the transfer tax.

They're also attractive for investors because there is no tax withholding of dividend payments from REICs. There is a 10% mandatory tax withholding from dividends pay by other types of companies.

And there's no withholding of taxes because dividends from REICs are not taxable income to private individual investors, and neither is their capital gains.

(Companies must pay taxes however.) They are exempt from the Large Property Tax.

Ever six months the Body of Sworn-In Valuers (BSV) evaluates the properties the REIC owns. The BSV also does an appraisal prior to the purchase of any property. The property's purchase price must be within 5% of the appraised amount.

A property must be held for a period of at least one year.

Economic Outlook for REICs in Greece

Greece got a lot of bad publicity recently due to the threat of its government failing to pay interest to owners of Greek government sovereign bonds. The economy has suffered from the financial crisis of 2007-2009.

Commercial rents have gone down a lot, and some commercial real estate properties may go on the market because of distress.

However, this may be an advantage for REICs, because they can raise additional capital in the capital markets, and can take advantage of the weakness of other real estate companies to pick up a lot of bargains.

This is how REITs really expanded in the United States in the early 1990s. They were able to buy up properties at a low cost because of the savings and loan crisis of the 1980s leading to the Resolution Trust Company.

However, the amount of net income distributed to REIC investors is relatively low. 80 to 90% is much more common.

Still, that's high considering the law requires them to distribute only 40%.

Real Estate Investment Companies in Greece have a lot of potential left to fulfill. As of this writing, there are only three. And two out of the three are subsidiaries of banks. And the third is in a strategic partnership with a financial group and its properties are described as mainly bank outlets. Clearly, the banks have found value in placing their branches in the hands of another company and leasing the space.

Greek REICs are:

Eurobank Properties REIC—commercial properties in four countries, but mainly Greece. http://www.eurobankproperties.gr/default.aspx?lang=en-US

Trastor REIC—first REIC formed and listed in Greece http://www.migre.gr/

MIG Real Estate REIC—office buildings and bank outlets and other buildings around Greece. http://www.trastor-reic.gr/Default.aspx?lang=2

Chapter Twenty-Three

Real Estate Investment Trusts in Nigeria

The Securities and Exchange Commission (SEC) of Nigeria released the first set of guidelines for Real Estate Investment Trusts in Nigeria (N-REITs) per the Investment and Securities Act (ISA) 2007.

The Central Bank of Nigeria (CBN) and the Debt Management Office (DMO) declared Asset Backed Securities (ABS) as exempt from taxes for ten years. N-REITs are Asset Backed Securities.

REITs in Nigeria can be either closed-end or open-end. They must have at least one hundred unitholders.

At least 75% of a closed-end REIT's assets must be in real estate. At least 70% of an open-end REIT's assets must be in real estate or real estate-related. None of their assets may be outside Nigeria.

At least 75% of their income must come from rents, mortgages or sale of property.

At least 90% of net income must be distributed to unit holders. Real Estate Investment Trusts in Nigeria are regulated by the SEC and the Federal Inland Revenue Service (FIRS).

The first established REIT was SkyeShelter Fund, but it lacked tax exemption.

Real Estate Investment Trusts in Nigeria (N-REITs):

Union Homes Plc REIT (UHOMREIT)—first REIT in Nigeria, launched September 2008, investing in mortgages http://www.unionhomes.com.ng/REIT.asp

SkyeShelter REIT (SKYESHELT)—rents out flats and houses
http://skyeshelterfund.com/

Chapter Twenty-Four

Real Estate Investment Trusts in Ghana

Real Estate Investment Trusts in Ghana began with "Collective Investment Schemes." These are governed by Securities Industry (Amendment) Law 2000, Act 590, but there must have been an earlier law. They are covered by the Securities and Exchange Commission - Ghana.

Collective investment schemes can be either mutual funds—much as we know them—or unit trusts, much as REITs in the US are trusts.

HFC Real Estate Investment Trust (HFC REIT) was started by HFC (then The Home Finance Company). In 1995 it was approved by the Bank of Ghana acting for the Securities and Exchange Commission.

Apparently it works to build houses and flats.

Hopefully in the future more REIT companies will form in Ghana.

Chapter Twenty-Five

Real Estate Investment Trusts in South Africa

Technically, there are no Real Estate Investment Trusts in South Africa. However, that country is included in the annual study of REITs around the world done by Ernst & Young, and it's included in a global REIT index.

This is because it does have some companies which, although not REITs in the full, ordinary sense of the term, are close enough to be included.

Many in South Africa who want the country to pass legislation enable full Real Estate Investment Trusts in South Africa.

Meanwhile, there are Portfolio Unit Trusts (PUT) that hold a portfolio of investment-grade properties and is listed on the JSE Limited (SA) in the Real Estate Sector.

They are governed by the Collective Investment Schemes Control Act No 45 of 2002 (Collective Investment Schemes Act).

PUTs are managed by a management company. They generally invest in shares of property companies. They can, but usually don't, invest directly in real estate properties.

The income they distribute to unit holders is not taxable, but any income they do not distribute is. But there are no minimum distribution requirements. The unit trust may choose to keep as much income as it's willing to pay taxes on.

A PUT cannot have more than 30% debt on the value of their underlying assets.

However, the appeal of REITs to ordinary income investors is the high dividends they are required to pay. Without a requirement to pay out large dividends, I cannot recommend Real Estate Investment Trusts in South Africa. Not they actually are that, and not Property Unit Trusts (PUTs).

Chapter Twenty-Six

Real Estate Investment Trusts in Israel

Real Estate Investment Trusts in Israel began January 2006.

Israeli REITs must be incorporated in Israel, and controlled and managed in Israel. Shares must be listed on the Tel Aviv Stock within twelve months of incorporation.

At least 75% of its assets must be profitable real estate investments. This must consist of at least 200 million NIS, and at least 75% must be invested in real estate located in Israel.

At least 90% of income must be distributed to shareholders on an annual basis, by April 30 of every year. Ownership of REIT shares must be so distributed under 50% is owned by four or fewer investors. Leverage (debt or gearing) is limited to 60% of total real estate property assets.

The first REIT in Israel to launch was called simply REIT 1, in 2006, from Excellence Nessuah.

Real Estate Trusts in Israel:

REIT 1

http://www.reit1.co.il/

Chapter Twenty-Seven

From our travel guidebook...

Shariah Compliant REITs

A substantial number of investors impose some form of moral, ethical, religious or political correctness "screen"—qualifications—on what kinds of companies they'll invest in.

Thus, peace activists don't buy the stock of defense contractors, PETA members don't buy stock in Hormel, and moral conservatives don't buy stock in casinos.

Unless they buy stock in companies with policies they dislike so they have the right to attend stock holder annual meetings and raise their issues.

Some people want to argue with this, saying that investors should just try to make as much money as possible no matter what because limiting your choices can restrict investing returns. If you want to promote some kind of cause, donate your extra wealth to an organization working for that cause.

I myself choose to operate along those lines, but I am not going to argue with those who believe in applying their personal principles to their investment decisions.

Therefore, it should come as no surprise devout Muslims might also wish to invest only in companies that do not operate against their religious beliefs. Apparently there are a lot of such investors, especially in the Gulf region—and that too should be no surprise. Nor should it be any surprise entrepreneurs in the Gulf Region and Southeast Asia are organizing shariah compliant REITs to attract money from those devout investors. The first REIT to actually be certified by the Gulf Council is in Singapore.

Businesses which conform to Muslim law are said to be shariah compliant.

Most of the types of businesses shariah-compliant Real Estate Investment Trusts must avoid include: tobacco, alcohol, pork, gambling and adult entertainment.

Interestingly, except for pork, both conservative Christians and socially conscious liberal left-wingers would agree with this list.

Shariah compliant REITs take their principles to the limit. Many socially conscious American investors might not see anything wrong with buying units of a REIT that owns shopping malls.

However, if the mall rents space to restaurants that serve pork dishes, a convenience store that sells cigarettes, a bar that serves alcoholic beverages, a movie theater that shows R rated movies, that REIT is not shariah compliant.

If a shariah compliant REIT owns a piece of property, they will not rent it out to any company that deals in any products or services forbidden by shariah law.

Where shariah compliance diverges from Christian and liberal socially conscious investments, is they must not have anything to do with collecting and charging interest. This makes the bank branches in that shopping mall just as abhorrent as the Hooters. It also means they cannot rent out office space to insurance companies.

The details of the regulations regarding interest get a little complicated. Therefore, to be shariah compliant, a REIT must have an Islamic Board attached to approve or disapprove all selections based on religion.

So there is a lot of extra red tape involved in getting things approved.

However, as mentioned, there are a lot of conservative Muslims who have money, who understand the value of real estate, who appreciate the advantages of REITs as a structure, but who don't want to receive dividends as a result of renting properties out to businesses making money through practices that offend their religious beliefs.

Many entrepreneurs in Singapore, which wants to be the REIT-capital of Asia, and which has a large Muslim Malay population as well as an intensely capitalistic Chinese population, want to invest that money. Singapore's Sabana Shari'ah Compliant Industrial Real Estate Investment Trust is the largest shariah compliant REIT in the world.

So do investors around the world. The first shariah-compliant REIT in the United Arab

Emirates is a joint venture with Eiffel Management, part of Societe de la Tour Eiffel, a French Real Estate Investment Trust.

So do entrepreneurs in the Gulf.

The Emirates REIT in The United Arab Emirates should go public sometime soon.

Shariah compliant REITs in Malaysia are also being studied by others seeking to duplicate them in other Muslim countries. One is an office and industrial REIT. Another one owns plantations for growing forests for palm oil.

Therefore, it's a good bet that this type of REIT is going to grow in numbers and popularity in the coming years.

Chapter Twenty-Eight

Real Estate Investment Trusts in The United Arab Emirates

There are no federal laws in the United Arab Emirates governing foreign ownership of real estate property assets. Each emirate makes its own policies.

In 2006, the Dubai International Financial Centre (which is a sort of free zone within Dubai) passed an Investment Trust Law and its Collective Investment Law No. 1, and an Investment Trust and REITs Rules Instrument. This got the ball rolling for Real Estate Investment Trusts in The United Arab Emirates (which includes Dubai).

One reason establishing them has been slow is there apparently are few taxes in the UAE, so the usual incentive of allowing a REIT to not pay taxes if they pay out at least ninety percent in dividends does not apply there.

Real Estate Investment Trusts are required to pay out at least eighty percent of net income to investors. Also REITs there can invest only in single ownership buildings, and in the UAE most residences are owned per unit. This means office and retail properties will be the main opportunity for REITs.

The First Real Estate Investment Trust in the Gulf Region

HSBC Bank Middle East Limited and asset manager Daman announced the formation of Arabian Real Estate Investment Trust (AREIT) January 28, 2006. It's the first Real Estate Investment Trust formed in the Gulf region.

It's managed by AREIT Management Ltd. It invests in prime commercial property throughout the Gulf Cooperation Council (GCC) region of Bahrain, Saudi Arabia, Kuwait, the United Arab Emirates, Oman and Qatar.

It is a private placement. It's not listed on any stock exchange. Therefore I wouldn't normally mention it, but it is of interest in revealing that the Gulf region is moving toward real estate companies, and therefore the demand for publicly traded REITs will grow. Their shareholders include Daman Asset Management, HSBC Bank Middle East Limited and Jazra Investments Limited.

Chairman of the Board of Directors and Independent Director is Robert McCuaig. They have offices in Dubai, Riyadh Saudi Arabia and Bahrain.

For one example, it bought the Wind Tower in Bahrain's Diplmatic Area in 2008, which is a landmark office building.

The Emirates REIT is the first Real Estate Investment Trust in The United Arab Emirates. It is managed by Emirates REIT Management.

http://emirates-reit.com/reit/

Abdulla Al Hamli is Chairman of Emirates REIT Management as well as CEO of the Dubai Islamic Bank, and is on the board of The Emirates REIT, as is Sylvain Vieujot, Deputy Chairman of Emirates REIT Management and CEO of Eiffel Management and Mark Inch Director of Emirates REIT Management and Chairman of Societe de la Tour Eiffel.

Its launch was announced November 23, 2010 by the Dubai Islamic Bank DISB.DU (DIB). It's a joint venture with Eiffel Management, connected with the Societe de la Tour Eiffel, a French Real Estate Investment Trust.

The Emirate REIT is Shariah compliant.

The Dubai Islamic Bank contributed seven seed properties to the portfolio. They all produce income and they're all debt-free. They are currently negotiating for fully let apartment buildings, office buildings and car parks. Investors will be able to obtain shares by trading them for their own income-producing real property assets, so that means soon to be former real estate investors and landlords will get many shares.

It will be based in the Dubai International Financial Center.

The Emirates REIT will be open to all investors, but fifty-one percent must come from the Gulf Cooperation Council. However, they have announced they should be listed on Dubai NASDAQ within a year.

At this time (July 2011), however, The Emirates REIT is not yet publicly listed.

During the real estate boom through 2007, Dubai was the biggest and fanciest property boom town in the world, exceeding even Las Vegas. Since the economic recession of 2008-2009, property values have fallen 62%. Even now, although foreign investment in the UAE is expected to go up, that's true for all economic sectors except real estate.

Chapter Twenty-Nine

Real Estate Investment Trusts in Kuwait

Real Estate Investment Trusts in Kuwait can be listed or private.

So far, the one REIT announced began in 2007. It's from Munshaat Real Estate Projects Co. K.S.C.C (MREP) , and it's Al Mahrab Tower REIT Real Estate Co. K.S.C.C. It was made a private placement at first, but planned to be listed by 2013. It is Sharia-compliant.

It was originally incorporated as a Kuwaiti closed shareholding company. It was formed for one project: The Al Mahrab Hotel tower. That's part of the Al Safwa Towers Project in Makkah. It's five towers on 9,635 square meters. It incorporates Islamic design elements, and will be located on Ajyad Street in Makkah Al Mukaramah fifty meters from the Haram. So it will offer a direct view of the Holy Kaaba. They planned to pay out 100% of income and capital gains, and expected a 24% rate of return.

Chapter Thirty

Real Estate Investment Trusts in Bahrain

On June 24, 2009 the Central Bank of Bahrain announced it had approved the first application for Real Estate Investment Trusts in Bahrain - under the Financial Trust Laws and Trust Laws of Bahrain - or Expert Collective Investment Undertaking.

Inovest REIT was established as a unit trust. Two Seas Trust is its trustee. It is Sharia-compliant, and listed on the Bahrain Stock Exchange.

Inovest Real Estate Investment Trust (IREIT)—a private REIT and Shariah compliant. http://www.inovest.bh/inovest_portfolio_new_oppportunities.asp

Chapter Thirty-One

Kazakhstan Real Estate Investment Trusts

I know there is at least one Real Estate Investment Trust in Kazakhstan.

However, I could not find out much about the law enabling this, except it seems to be based on the US REIT model.

The one Real Estate Investment Trust in Kazakhstan:

Velikaya Stena

Chapter Thirty-Two

Real Estate Investment Trusts in Pakistan

J
uly 26, 2007 the Securities and Exchange Commission of Pakistan (REITS & New Initiatives Wing & Specialized Companies Division) announced they were introducing the concept of Real Estate Investment Trusts in Pakistan. On January 31, 2008 they issued rules for establishing REITs under issued Real Estate Investment Trust Regulations, 2008 (S.R.O. 94(I)/ 2008, making them a specialized investment vehicle. This was announced February 6, 2008.

Apparently they did not require a separate law to do this, as is usual for countries just starting with REITs. Instead, they cite the authority granted to them by sub-section (2) of section 282B of the Companies Ordinance, 1984 (XLVII of 1984).

Legal Rules for Real Estate Investment Trusts in Pakistan

In Pakistan, REITs are required to adhere to the trust structure. The properties belong to the unit holders, vested in the name of the name of the trustee, with the REIT management company (RMC) managing them in trust for the unit holders. The RMC must have at least a 20% stake in the company, and a maximum of 50%, and does receive management fees. REITs do not pay taxes so long as they distribute 90% of profits to shareholders. They do plan to allow full foreign ownership and repatriation of profits. They must own at least 5 billion rupees worth of properties. They are currently allowed to operate only in allowed in Islamabad/Rawalpindi, Karachi, Lahore, Peshawar and Quetta.

To encourage the formation of REITs, the government gave real estate owners who sell properties to a REIT a tax holiday through 2010.

In addition to the REIT Management Companies (RMC) there are specific project known as REIT "Schemes." (Evidently, in Pakistan English the word "scheme" does not have the same negative connotation it does in the United States.)

There are two types of REIT Schemes. They are Developmental and Rental.

After completing a development project (which may be industrial, residential or commercial), through construction or refurbishment, it is sold. Those companies distribute the profits to the unit holders.

Rental REIT Schemes own and manage rental properties (commercial real estate or residential) on behalf of unitholders, who receive a stream of dividends from the dividends from rental profits.

I'm not sure why they thought requiring developmental projects to be limited was a good idea. Income investors will be interested only in Rental REIT Schemes.

Pakistan studied the beginning of Real Estate Investment Trusts in Malaysia. In 2009 the SECP reduced the stamp duty and registration fee for REIT properties in Punjab and Sindh provinces. In Punjab it was reduced from 2% to 0.5%. In Sindh it was reduced from 3% to 0.5%.

REITs in Pakistan are Just Beginning

The SECP received four initial requests to form Real Estate Investment Trust management companies in Pakistan, and took a year to scrutinize them. Two of those were rejected for failure to meet regulatory requirements. They must have at least 50 million rupees at the time of application. Within thirty working days of the registration of the REIT Scheme, they must increase their capital to at least five hundred million rupees.

However, two companies were approved: Arif Habib REIT Management Company Limited and AKD REIT Management Company Limited. Arif Habib and Akeel Karim Dhedi (AKD) are two of the country's leading stockbrokers.

Arif Habib is part of a larger holding company which is still forming and promoting more Real Estate Investment Trusts in Pakistan. Mr Habib said in a December 2010 interview he expected his REITs to invest mainly in social and low-cost housing because there is a shortage of good living spaces in the country. He also said he expected medium term returns (from 3 to 7 years) to average 30%.

He expected to get the first REIT actually launched early in 2011, though as of this writing it hasn't happened. It will be based in the port city of Karachi.

It's encouraging the process of forming REITs in Pakistan is moving forward. A study done in

2005 found the picture for real estate investment in Pakistan rather discouraging. It produced low returns (from 3 to 5% - negative in real terms). The law favored tenants, making it hard to foreclose on them when necessary. Recording of property ownership was not kept up, so many times two different parties claimed ownership to the same tract of land.

Yet Pakistan has a large population, most of them very poor, and large shortages of affordable housing. The home construction industry could not keep up with the need. Therefore, the government is hoping having publicly listed companies in the real estate markets will help make them more efficient, providing more housing to the population, partly by attracting foreign—especially Gulf region—investment. Net foreign investment in Pakistan has fallen dramatically in They also hope those Pakistani citizens who can afford to invest will do so, providing them with additional revenue from dividends. They also wish for greater transparency, because according to news accounts, their real estate sector has a lot of corruption, including major scandals.

Hopefully, there will be Real Estate Investment Trusts in Pakistan soon, and everyone from the organizers, the investors and the tenants will benefit.

Chapter Thirty-Three

Real Estate Investment Trusts in Thailand

On October 11, 2010, the Securities and Exchange Commission of Thailand approved a regulatory framework for Real Estate Investment Trusts in Thailand. This began with passage of the Trust for Transactions in Capital Market Act BE 2550 (2007).

REITs will be actual trusts. They will be managed by REIT management companies, regulated by the SEC of Thailand and appointed by the trustee. They will in effect replace the Property Fund for Public Offering (PFPO) structure which was established in 2002 to deal with distressed assets in the wake of the 1997 financial crisis.

They are allowed to leverage up to fifty percent of the value of their assets. They may invest in a wide range of real estate properties, barring only those that are illegal or immoral. Investors buy trust certificates. Once the trust is established, it must be listed on the Thai Stock Exchange (SET) within 60 days. They must have capital of at least 500 hundred million baht.

No one person or related group of persons may hold more than 50% of the certificates. Foreign ownership of trust certificates is limited to 49% of the total. Their investments in real estate properties must be at least 75% of total assets. They may not invest in property less than 80% completed, so Thailand has chosen to restrict them from developing property. When they do, they must hold it for a period of at least one year.

They must pay out at least 90% of profits on an annual basis. As of March 22, 2011 the Thai government has announced it is delaying implementation of the REITs in Thailand law while the Revenue Department reviews it.

Hopefully that process will be completed quickly, and soon Real Estate Investment Trusts in Thailand will be a reality.

Chapter Thirty-Four

Real Estate Investment Trusts in Malaysia

Listed Property Trusts - M-REIT

Malaysia was the first country in Asia to adopt rules creating Real Estate Investment Trusts. That happened in 1986 when Bank Negara Malaysia (Central Bank of Malaysia) approved a regulatory framework based on the Companies Act 1965 and the Securities Industry Act 1983. They are also referred to as listed property trusts (actually, private unlisted trusts are also allowed), and they're formed as Malaysian registered trusts.

The first Malaysian REIT, Arab Malaysian First Property Trust, launched September 1989.

The guidelines for listed property trusts were issued by the Securities Commission in 1991, and revised in 1995.

In 1999 the Securities Commission examined Real Estate Investment Trusts in other countries such as the United States, and issued two papers: Consultation Paper on Property Trust Fund (1999) and Consultation Paper on Property Trust Funds and Real Estate Investment Trusts (2002). Then came the Finance Act 2004. On January 3, 2005 the Securities Commission issued Guidelines on Real Estate Investment Trusts.

On November 22, 2005 the Securities Commission issued Guidelines on Islamic Real Estate Investment Trusts (Islamic REITs). This makes Malaysia a leader in the growing trend in the Middle East and Asia of shariah-compliant REITs.

REITs in Malaysia must pay out at least 90% of their income to shareholders to avoid taxation.

REITs Around the World

M-REITs are exempt from paying stamp duty when they sell property. And property owners who sell to listed property trusts are exempt from capital gains taxes.

Dividends to nonresidents must have 20% withheld for their taxes effective 2012.

M-REITs in Malaysia must be managed and administered by a management company approved by the Securities Commission. The Securities Commission must also approve its choice of trustee.

The management company is limited to owning no more than 70% of the equity, together with that owned by foreign investors (foreign effective equity). Local investors (Bumiputra) must own at least 30% of the fund.

The minimum fund size is RM100 million. The property it owns must be run by a qualified property manager.

At least 50% of the trust's total assets must be invested in real estate. It can invest up to 25% of assets into cash and money market funds.

The fund cannot invest more than 5% of assets into the securities of any one issuer. And it must not invest more than 10% into the securities of any group of companies.

Various REITs were listed in the 1990s, but by 2005 only three were still on the stock exchange. But since the new rules announced by the Securities Exchange, more have been launched.

Real Estate Investment Trusts in Malaysia (M-REITs):

1. Starhill REIT—owns two hotels
http://www.starhillreit.com/

2. Amanah Raya REIT—offices, schools, industrial and retail
http://www.arrm.com.my/

3. Axis Real Estate Investment Trust—Islamic office and industrial properties
http://www.axis-reit.com.my/

4. Tower Real Estate Investment Trust—3 office buildings
http://www.tower-reit.com.my

5. AmFIRST REIT—retail, offices and hotel properties in Klang Valley
http://www.amfirstreit.com.my/

6. Al-Hadharah Boustead REIT—palm oil plantations
http://www.al-hadharahboustead.com.my/overview.html

7. Amanah Harta Tanah PNB

8. Amanah Harta Tanah PNB 2

9. Al-Aqar KPJ REIT—healthcare properties
http://www.alaqarkpjreit.com.my/

10. Hektar REIT—first Malaysian REIT focusing only on retail sector
http://www.hektarreit.com/

11. UOA Real Estate Investment Trust—assembles parcels of commercial properties
http://www.uoareit.com.my/

12. Quill Capita Trust—retail properties
http://www.qct.com.my/

13. Atrium Real Estate Investment Trust—logistics properties
http://www.atriumreit.com.my/

14. Sunway REIT - Malaysian REIT
http://www.sunwayreit.com/

15. CapitaMalls Malaysia Trust—shopping malls
http://www.capitamallsmalaysia.com/

So Real Estate Investment Trusts in Malaysia are gaining ground, and should continue to prosper. The shariah compliant ones are being used as a model in other Islamic countries.

Chapter Thirty-Five

Real Estate Investment Trusts in Singapore - S-REITs

The first Real Estate Investment Trust in Singapore, known as S-REIT, was CapitaMall Trust in 2002. They're regulated as Collective Investment Schemes or Business Trusts under the Monetary Authority of Singapore's Code on Collective Investment Schemes, and are structured as unit trusts. They're called an S-REIT to distinguish them from other countries.

The manager of an S-REIT should be a corporation with a physical location in Singapore and a capitalization of at least $1 million (Singapore dollars). REIT trustees must be approved by the Monetary Authority of Singapore. At least 25% of their units must be held by at least 500 public shareowners.

The Singapore government is hoping to make it a major Asian Real Estate Investments Trusts center, including for cross-border REITs. Foreign S-REIT investors are subject to only 10% withholding on their dividends. When an S-REIT buys a building in Singapore, it's not subject to stamp duty.

Many S-REITs invest in property outside of Singapore. As of June 2007, 21% of S-REIT property value was in real estate outside of Singapore - in a total of ten other countries. This is relatively high. In many countries, the REIT laws encourage these property companies to invest within their own country. However, while Singapore is a big city it's a small country, so it may not want REITs bidding up real estate property values when bargains are available in other places.

S-REITs are Legal Trusts

Singapore is the only REIT country in the world having REITs pay unit holders 100% of cash flows. In the United States and most other countries, it's 90%.

The structure of S-REITs reminds me of Master Limited Partnerships in the United States. That's because they are externally managed by a company which is a wholly owned subsidiary of a real estate corporation. This leads me to conclude S-REITs give these corporations a business structure a large tax break.

In 2007 they passed legislation enacted by the Monetary Authority of Singapore (MAS) which enhances disclosure on short-term yield enhancing arrangements - financial engineering. It discourages arrangements to entrench a manager's position and disallows discounts to institutional investors at IPO. It also increases the minimum threshold for investment in real estate—an S-REIT must have at least 75% of its assets in income-producing real estate.

And no more than 10% of a REIT's revenue can come from nonrental income.

Singapore's Securities Industry Council (SIC) extended the takeover and merger code to make it easier for one REIT to buy up another.

S-REITs are sector specific, focusing on retail, office, industrial, hotels, residential and medical properties.

Singapore Real Estate Investment Trusts:

CapitaMall Trust—one of the largest S-REITs in Singapore, and the second listed on the exchange
http://www.capitamall.com/home.html

CapitaCommercial Trust—one of the largest S-REITs in Singapore, the 2nd ever listed on their stock exchange
http://www.cct.com.sg/

CapitaRetail China Trust—the first public REIT in Singapore to hold a property portfolio exclusively of retail shopping malls in China
http://www.capitaretailchina.com/

Starhill Global Trust—buying properties all around Asia
http://www.starhillglobalreit.com/

Ascendas Real Estate Investment Trust—first space and logistics S-REIT in Singapore
http://www.a-reit.com/

Ascendas India Trust—this is a trust which owns industrial parks in some areas of India

REITs Around the World

http://www.a-itrust.com/

Mapletree Logistics Trust—space and logistics properties in Singapore, Malaysia, Vietnam, Japan, Hong Kong, China and Korea
http://www.mapletreelogisticstrust.com/

Sabana REIT—world's largest sharia-compliant REIT, launched in 2010
http://www.sabana-reit.com/index.html

Ascott Residence Trust—owner-operator of serviced residences in twelve countries of Asia and Europe
http://www.ascottreit.com/

Suntec REIT—owns offices and retail space in Singapore
http://www.suntecreit.com/

Cambridge Industrial Trust—owns over 40 industrial properties in Singapore
http://www.cambridge-itrust.com/phoenix.zhtml?c=196153&p=homepage

ParkWayLife REIT—owns 3 hospitals in Singapore and 39 nursing homes in Japan
http://www.plifereit.com/

First REIT—owns hospitals and nursing homes mainly in Indonesia
http://www.first-reit.com/index.html

AIMS AMP Capital Industrial REIT—owns hospitals and nursing homes mainly in Indonesia
http://www.aimsampcapital.com/AAC/EN/Default.aspx

Fraser's Commercial Trust—owns high end office buildings in Singapore, Japan and Australia
http://www.fraserscommercialtrust.com/home

Lippo-Mapletree Indonesia Retail Trust—invests in shopping malls in Indonesia
http://www.lmir-trust.com/

CDL Hospitality Trusts—owns hotels, mainly in Singapore
http://www.cdlht.com/

SaizenREIT—owns many residential properties in Japan
http://www.saizenreit.com.sg/

Fortune REIT—owns 14 shopping malls in Hong Kong
http://www.fortunereit.com/eng/index.php

Cache Logistics Trust—owns 8 warehouses in Singapore
http://www.cache-reit.com/

IndiaBulls Properties Investment Trust—owns commercial and residential properties in Mumbai India

K-REIT Asia—owns quality retail and office properties in Singapore and Australia
http://www.kreitasia.com/

Therefore, S-REITs (Singapore Real Estate Investment Trusts) are a great way to profit from economic activity in much of Asia.

Chapter Thirty-Six

From our travel brochure...

Investing in Property Outside Your Own Country—Good or Bad Idea?

Something struck me while I was researching the web site of one of Singapore's S-REITs. They own A LOT of residential properties, apartment houses and so on—in Japan.

I realized, through owning shares in that company, a lot of people in Singapore (and probably other places) were receiving income from ordinary Japanese people paying their rent. You may have noticed by now a lot of countries (not all, but a lot) do not allow their REITs to buy properties outside that country. Obviously, they want to keep investment capital within their own borders to help their domestic real estate industry - but what about the income that capital generates? They're losing out. Yes, capital leaves that country when a REIT buys a property in another country, but once the REIT starts receiving income from that property, the money flows back to the parent country.

Another REIT in Singapore owns a huge number of logistics facilities in China and Japan. Its shareholders in Singapore or wherever they live, are receiving a piece of all the exports and imports of those two countries. Given both are extremely export-oriented economies which also need to import a lot of natural resources, and both have a lot of sea coasts and harbor facilities, this is gigantic. And local investors in the REIT can take the dividend income they're receiving from foreign properties and help their local real estate economy by paying their mortgages or rent, buying more food at the local supermarket, shopping at their local mall, and so on.

Restricting capital may seem to make sense, but it's short-term, limited thinking.

Chapter Thirty-Seven

Real Estate Investment Trusts in Hong Kong

Hong Kong first published its REIT rules in August 2003. They are considered collective investment schemes under Section 104 of the Securities and Futures Ordinance (Chapter 571 of the Laws of Hong Kong).

Hong Kong Real Estate Investment Trusts listed on the stock exchange since December 2005, with the beginning of The Link REIT from the Hong Kong Housing Authority.

The Link REIT is now one of the world's largest REITs.

Hong Kong REITs are Critical Because in Hong Kong, Real Estate is in Short Supply

Real estate has always been a big industry in Hong Kong for the simple reason the country is just one city and, until 1997, separated from greater China behind it. Therefore, it could not expand anywhere except up.

Residential areas and shopping centers are packed. Traffic is extremely congested.

So now the real estate market in Hong Kong is considered one of the most mature in the world, but is still volatile. And Hong Kong is one of the most transparent stock exchanges.

They must pay out at least 90% of their net profits to shareholders as dividends. They must have three or more properties in their portfolio which are now owner-occupied.

At least 75% of their assets must be in real estate, government securities or cash.

REITs Around the World

At least 75% of their income must come from rent, mortgages or sale of properties.

They may invest in foreign property, but may not use more than 45% leverage or loan to value ratio. And if they wish to do a joint venture, they must own at least 50% of the property.

Only 10% in property development is allowed. The REIT does pay the property taxes.

Management is required to be external.

REITs in Hong Kong do not pay any taxes on the 90% they distribute to shareholders. However, they do pay corporate taxes on the 10% they do not distribute.

Hong Kong Real Estate Investment Trusts:

The Link REIT—one of largest REITs in the world.
http://www.thelinkreit.com/EN/Pages/default.aspx

Sunlight REIT—office and retail properties in Hong Kong.
http://www.sunlightreit.com/en/

Regal REIT—Regal hotels in Hong Kong.
http://www.regalreit.com/index.html

Champion REIT—office and retail properties in Hong Kong
http://www.championreit.com/html/eng/main_intro.jsp

GZI REIT—residential properties in Hong Kong.
http://www.gzireit.com.hk/eng/pindex.asp

Hui Xian REIT—owns Oriental Plaza in Beijing
http://www.hkrei.com/reit/hui-xian-reit/

Prosperity REIT—owns office buildings in Hong Kong.
http://www.prosperityreit.com/eng/index.php

Fortune REIT—fourteen shopping malls in Hong Kong.
http://www.fortunereit.com/eng/index.php

Therefore, Hong Kong Real Estate Investment Trusts are a terrific way to profit from investing in Hong Kong's economic activity.

Chapter Thirty-Eight

Real Estate Investment Trusts in The Philippines - P-REITs

The Philippines authorized the creation of Real Estate Investment Trusts with passage of The Real Estate Investment Trust Act December 17, 2009. It's known as The REIT Law (Republic Act No. 9856). These are being termed a P-REIT.

However, before any REITs can actually be started, or existing real estate companies change their status, The Bureau of Internal Revenue (BIR) must write a Revenue Regulation (RR).

Based on the law a REIT in The Philippines must own real estate property assets that generate income. It must be registered as a corporation in The Philippines and listed with The Philippines Stock Exchange (PSE).

It must have beginning capital, of cash or property, of at least 300 million pesos. If the REIT is going to own only buildings it can be up to 100% foreign owned. If it's to own land, foreign ownership is limited to 40%.

It must have at least 1,000 public shareholders who own at least 50 shares each, and who own a total of at least one-third of the outstanding shares. These shareowners are defined as not being associated of REIT sponsors.

The higher of one-third or two members of the Board of Directors must be independent.

REITs in The Philippines will be required to distribute at least 90% of distributable income as dividends on an annual basis - as cash, stock or property dividends. They do not pay taxes on distributed dividends.

Shareholders residing in inside the republic must pay 10% taxes, but overseas Filipinos, including overseas contract workers, do not pay any taxes. However, nonresident shareowners are subject to a withholding tax of 10%.

REITs in The Philippines Must Obey Complex Rules

They can invest in property inside or outside The Philippines, but at least thirty-five percent of their portfolio must consist of property inside the Philippines. Investment in property outside The Philippines is limited to 40%. Up to twenty-five percent of their capital may consist of ordinary investments such as cash, stocks and bonds, except they may not own shares in listed property company. And no more than 15% of this may be held in any issuer's securities, unless that's The Philippines government. They may put up to 25% of this capital into government bonds.

Property acquired by REITs listed on The Philippines Stock Exchange must have a good track record for at least three years prior to their acquisition.

They may not develop property unless they hold it for at least three years. They may not leverage more than 35% of its market value.

P-REITs must have an external fund and property manager, and there are rules to ensure their independence and competence.

As of this writing, some of The Philippines' biggest real estate companies and its two leading mall owners are planning to convert to REIT status when the tax rulings are issued: Ayala Land, Filinvest Land, Ortigas and Co, SM Prime Holdings, and Robinson's Land.

Chapter Thirty-Nine

Real Estate Investment Trusts in Taiwan

Real Estate Investment Trusts in Taiwan began with work on the Real Estate Securitization Law in 2002, which passed July 23, 2003. Businesses or financial institutions can set up trusts to own and operate real estate properties. They can be private or public.

The first one got started in 2004 and was listed on the Taiwan Stock Exchange March 10, 2005.

Minimum initial capital ranges from NT$ 300 million to NT$ 2 billion depending on the scope of their plan.

After funds are raised in the Initial Public Offering, they're used to buy properties with stable incomes from rent. They're prohibited from buying properties without stable rental income. The trustee, which must be a publicly listed company, can manage the properties or hire an outside management company.

They are in effect closed end funds for real estate investment, because after the IPO they cannot raise funds by selling additional shares.

The REIT must pay out at least 90% of income annually in return for paying no income taxes. REIT shareholders pay the lowest rate of taxes on the dividends, 10%, and that is withheld from the dividend payment. 10% is the rate of taxes the individual investor must pay on the dividends from REITs they receive. This is true no matter what their ordinary marginal tax rate is.

At least 75% of the trust's assets must be in real estate assets. REITs can invest up to 20% of their assets in short term commercial paper, bank deposits, government bonds and such. The trustee may borrow up to 35% of the net value of the trust's assets.

There should be at least 50 unit holders, a unit holder may now own over 50% of the REIT's units unless they are independent professional investors.

There have been no IPOs of REITs in Taiwan for over three years. Late in 2010, investors approved the liquidation of two REITs, the San Tin and Kee Tai Star. This is a poor trend that hopefully will be reversed soon.

Real Estate Investment Trusts in Taiwan:

FuBon REIT No. #1

Trident REIT

Gallop REIT No. #1

Cathay REIT #1

Shin Kong REIT #1

Fubon REIT #2

Cathay REIT #2

Chapter Forty

Real Estate Investment Trusts in South Korea

REITs in South Korea began with Real Estate Investment Company Act (REICA) in 2001. The Act on Administration and Promotion of Real Estate Development Business (REDBA) of December 2007 regulates collective investment vehicles such as REITs. Real Estate Investment Trusts in South Korea have a closed end corporate structure. They must be established as joint stock companies—chusik hoesa in Korean—and publicly listed on the Korean Stock Exchange.

There are three kinds of REITs in South Korea:

Self-Managed REITs (S-REITs)—they invest in properties and manage the real estate themselves.

Manager-Entrusted REITs (M-REITs)—Their business is conducted by an outside manager.

(The two of the above together are referred to as K-REITs.)

Corporate Restructuring REITs (CR-REITs)—handle the corporate restructuring of companies that own real estate.

Starting in 2008, there's a specialized kind of DS-REIT which is allowed to invest all funds into real estate development and to remain privately held instead of publicly listed.

They must obtain authorization from the Ministry of Transport and Maritime Affairs. They may have an internal or external manager.

REITs Around the World

They must invest at least 80% of their assets in real estate related assets. They are permitted to invest up to 30% for property development. They not hold more than 10% of voting securities of another business. At least 10% total assets must be either real estate or cash equivalents. They can buy, manage, improve, rent out and sell real estate.

Minimum capital requirements is KRW 1 billion, with 10 billion within six months. Within six months of obtaining approval, they must offer at least 30% of shares to the public. There are no geographical restrictions on where their properties are. They may not borrow money, except in the short term to manage their cash flow. One shareholder can own no more than 30% of a REIT in South Korea.

They are required to distribute 90% of their income once more year. Their own income, however, is still subject to corporate taxes. Long term debt cannot exceed double the net equity value without shareholder approval.

Foreign investment is allowed. In 2008 the investment banker Macquarie Bank set up the first entirely foreign owned REIT in South Korea.

Real Estate Investment Trusts in South Korea:

1. Realty Korea 1

2. Ures-Meritz 1

3. KORAMCO Reits and Trusts forms various REIT funds usually under KOCREF

4. Macquarie Central Office

5. C9 Infinity

6. Macquarie NPS

7. KR-1

8. KR2 DS-REIT

9. Infinity NPS 1

10. Dasan S-REIT

Chapter Forty-One

Real Estate Investment Trusts in Japan J-REITs

J-REIT is the acronym for Japanese Real Estate Investment Trusts.

REITs were created by the Japanese government in November 2000. They are corporations traded on the Tokyo Stock Exchange and are regulated according to the Law - Investment Trust and Investment Company. They are considered an investment company under LITIC.

On September 10, 2001, Nippon Building Fund Inc and Japan Real Estate Investment Corporation became the first Japanese REITs to be listed. There are currently a total of 35.

J-REITs are Important in a Small, Wealthy Country

Japan is a small, crowded country, so real estate is important to its people and economy. During the late 1980s when Japan was booming, the extremely high cost of real estate was used as an indicator of its irrationality. Just a small area of downtown Tokyo had a market price higher than the entire state of California USA. Its economy and stock market did crash in 1990.

Japanese REITs were hit hard by the 2007-2009 financial crisis when property values were again driven down.

Just recently, the Bank of Japan announced it was buying up assets, and this would include buying up 60 billion yen of JREITs.

However, the creation of the JREIT may have helped contribute to an improvement in Japanese real estate values since they peaked in the early 1990s. That's because they opened the real estate sector up to new sources of financing.

Japanese J-REITs can sell bonds, and recently have been more successful at this, though during the prior two years of the financial crisis they could not sell many bonds.

In May 2008 Japanese law was changed to allow JREITs to buy property outside Japan, but so far they haven't done so.

The Investment and Trust Law created two different legal systems for a REIT in Japan: Investment Corporation System and Investment Trust System.

Right now, all JREITs listed are under the Investment Corporation System. They are required to pay out at least 90% of income to shareholders.

They may own commercial properties. Office buildings are common, then shopping centers and other commercial real estate forms such as hotels and logistics. Surprisingly, few REITs specialize in retail properties, especially shopping centers, even though Japan is no doubt the trendiest country in Asia.

The most widely held form of asset by JREITs is residential. This includes all kinds of apartments, plus student and senior housing. This makes sense in that the Japanese have had to cut back on shopping, but must still live somewhere. And buying a house in an urban area is extremely expensive. So most Japanese must rent apartments.

They are structured as a special purpose investment vehicle. Such functions as property management and administration are outsourced. Asset management firms handle their property portfolios. So they all have an Asset Manager.

They may engage only in the real estate business. At least 50% of their assets must be stable, cash-generating properties, and at least 70% of their assets must be real estate. Including real estate certificates, at least 95% of their assets must be in real estate. They may not develop properties.

They must have total capital of at least 5 billion yen, and at least 1 billion of net equity.

J-REITs are not allowed to have subsidiaries. They may not own more than 50% of another company. They may not borrow money from anyone except a qualified institutional investor.

They are required to withhold 20% for taxes from distributions made to shareholders.

J-REITs currently are:

1. Starts Proceed Investment Corporation—rental properties
http://www.sp-inv.co.jp/

2. Advance Residence Investment Corporation—many residential units
http://www.adr-reit.com/en/

3. Industrial & Infrastructure Fund Investment Corporation—industrial and logistics properties
http://www.iif-reit.com/english/

4. Nomura Real Estate Residential Fund, Inc.—many residential properties
http://www.nre-rf.co.jp/english/

5. Mori Hills REIT Investment Corporation—urban redevelopment programs
http://www.mori-hills-reit.co.jp/en/

6. Nippon Commercial Investment Corporation
7. MID REIT, Inc.—office buildings in Osaka
http://www.midreit.jp/eng/outline/index4.html

8. Nippon Accommodations Fund Inc.—many different kinds of residential properties
http://www.naf-r.jp/english/index.html

9. Invincible Investment Corporation—diversified, even owns parking lots
http://www.invincible-inv.co.jp/eng/

10. Japan Excellent, Inc.—office buildings
http://www.excellent-reit.co.jp/eng/

11. Japan Rental Housing Investments Inc.—many urban residential properties
http://www.jrhi.co.jp/en/

12. Nippon Hotel Fund Investment Corporation—hotel industry
http://www.nhf-reit.co.jp/

13. BLife Investment Corporation—residential and retail
http://www.blife-reit.co.jp/eng/

14. Top REIT, Inc.—apartments, retail and offices
http://www.top-reit.co.jp/english/

15. Japan Hotel and Resort, Inc.—hotels and resorts
http://www.jhrth.com/eng/

16. Hankyu REIT, Inc.—urban properties
http://www.hankyu-reit.jp/eng/

17. Daiwa Office Investment Corporation—office buildings
http://www.daiwa-office.co.jp/en/index.html

18. FC Residential Investment Corporation—residential properties
http://www.fcric.co.jp/

19. Sekisui House SI Investment Corporation—residential and shopping
http://www.shsi-reit.co.jp/eng/

20. Kenedix Realty Investment Corporation—midsized office buildings
http://www.kdx-reit.com/eng/

21. Fukuoka REIT Corporation—Kyushu area
http://www.fukuoka-reit.jp/eng/

22. Japan Logistics Fund, Inc.—logistics/warehouses
http://8967.jp/eng/

23. Heiwa Real Estate REIT,Inc.—many commercial properties
http://www.heiwa-re.co.jp/english/

24. Frontier Real Estate Investment Corporation—shopping centers
http://www.frontier-reit.co.jp/eng/

25. MORI TRUST Sogo Reit, Inc.—office buildings in Tokyo
http://www.mt-reit.jp/english/

26. United Urban Investment Corporation—diversified REIT
http://www.united-reit.co.jp/eng/outline/index7.html

27. Nomura Real Estate Office Fund, Inc.—owns and operates office buildings
http://www.nre-of.co.jp/english/

28. Global One Real Estate Investment Corporation - Class A office buildings
http://www.go-reit.co.jp/eng/

29. TOKYU REIT, Inc.—office buildings and residential properties
http://www.tokyu-reit.co.jp/eng/index.html

30. Premier Investment Company—office and retail in Tokyo Economic Block
http://www.pic-reit.co.jp/en/index.html

31. Japan Prime Realty Investment Corporation—office and retail properties in Central Business District of Tokyo
http://www.jpr-reit.co.jp/jpr_e/

32. ORIX JREIT Inc.—diversified REIT
http://www.orixjreit.com/english/

33. Japan Retail Fund Investment Corporation—many retail properties
http://www.jrf-reit.com/english/index.html

34. Japan Real Estate Investment Corporation—office buildings
http://www.j-re.co.jp/english/

35. Nippon Building Fund Inc.—many residential properties
http://www.nbf-m.com/nbf_e/

Chapter Forty-Two

Real Estate Investment Trusts in Australia

A-REITs

The government of Australia began allowing real estate investment trusts in that country in 1971, making it one of the first countries to have them after the United States. The first one listed on the Australian Securities Exchange (ASX) was Property Trust (LPT).

Up until March 2008, publicly listed REITs in Australia were known as Listed Property Trusts (LPTs). This terminology distinguished them from privately held REITs, known as Unlisted Property Trusts.

Real Estate Investment Trusts are Big in Australia

In that month, they were re-termed Australian Real Estate Investment Trusts (A-REITs). There're now more than 60 A-REITs listed on the Melbourne exchange, making Australia the country with the second largest number of REITs, behind the United States but ahead of Canada. They account for fully 12% of the world's listed real estate.

A-REITs can also be listed on The Bendigo Stock Exchange, the Newcastle Stock Exchange, and the Australia Pacific Exchange.

Australian REITs are allowed to hold property in or outside of Australia. The most popular countries for them, outside Australia itself, are the United States, New Zealand and The United Kingdom.

They are measured by what is term their Net Tangible Assets (NTA), which is the balance sheet total of their properties.

Most A-REITs contract management duties to outside third parties.

A-REITs can choose to adopt one of two structures. Stand-alone trusts provide investors pure exposure to the underlying real estate portfolio. Stapled securities provide investors exposure to a funds management and/or property development company besides the real estate portfolio.

If they provide purely exposure to the underlying real estate portfolio, as equity REITs in the United States do, they are an A-REIT that's a trust similar to all REITs in the U.S.

Stapled REITs are investment vehicles which actually include two or more separate but related entities. They actually have separate units, but those don't trade separately—they're stapled together, so to speak. You can buy and sell only the overall entity.

It's often the case with stapled A-REITs one company owns and operates real estate as U.S. equity REITs do, while one or more companies issue investment funds which are like small mutual funds which invest in real estate portfolios put together by the entity.

U.S. REITs used to have the staple structure, but Congress felt this violated the spirit of the REIT tax preference treatment and outlawed it in 1984, though some were grandfathered.

I am no fan of actively traded mutual funds, so I have no desire to wish to indirectly purchase shares in one devoted to real estate when I really just want to invest in the REIT's property portfolio and reap my share of the profits.

Many of the funds are invested in other A-REITs. You can do that by yourself, without paying an extra layer of management fees to somebody in another A-REIT.

There're Five Basic Kinds of Australian REITs:

Industrial

Office

Hotel / Leisure

Retail

Diversified - investment in a mixture of Industrial, Office, Hotel and Retail

All A-REITs must have a Responsible Entity (RE). That's a term of Australian law created by the Managed Investments Act July 1, 1998.

Usually, managed investment schemes have a trustee to hold it in trust for the trust owners and a manager—a double tier system.

In Australia the trustee and manager are both replaced by the simple Responsible Entity, which must be an Australian public company holding a dealer's license to act as an RE. It must have at least net tangible assets of $50,000. If it has under $5 million it must appoint a custodian.

A Responsible Entity Replaces the "Prescribed Interests" Regime

The law places many responsibilities and duties on them, and imposes civil penalties of up to $1 million for violating them. $200,000 in penalties for its officers.

Real Estate Trusts in Australia—A-REITs

Ardent Leisure Group—leisure properties
http://www.ardentleisure.com.au/

Abacus Property Group—acquires and manages real estate properties
http://www.abacusproperty.com.au/

Agricultural Land Trust—farmland in Australia
http://www.asx.com.au/asx/research/companyInfo.do?by=asxCode&asxCode=agj

Astro Japan Property—commercial properties in Japan
http://www.astrojapanproperty.com/

ALE Property Group—landlord for Australian pubs
http://www.alegroup.com.au/irm/content/home.html

APN European Retail—commercial properties in Australia and Europe
http://www.apngroup.com.au/

Aspen Group—diversified stapled A-REIT with commercial properties
http://www.aspengroup.com.au/

Australand Group—land development
http://www.australand.com.au/

Australian Education Trust—a daycare centers in Australia
http://www.educationtrust.com.au/home.aspx

Babcock & Brown Residential Land Partners—land development projects
http://www.bbresidentiallandpartners.com/

Becton Property Group—property development and funds management
http://www.becton.com.au/html/index.asp

Bunnings Warehouse—warehouse type store popular in Australia
http://www.bwptrust.com.au/

Carindale Property—Carindale Westfield shopping center
http://www.carindalepropertytrust.com.au/carindalepropertytrust

Centro Properties Group—shopping centers in Australia, New Zealand and the United States
http://www.centro.com.au/

CFS Retail Property Trust—regional and subregional shopping malls in Australia
http://www.colonialfirststate.com.au/cfx/

Challenger Diversified Property—diversified retail properties
http://www.challenger.com.au/listed/cdi/cdi.asp

Challenger Kenedix Japan Trust—retail real estate in Japan
http://www.challenger.com.au/listed/ckt/ckt.asp

Challenger Wine Trust—Australian vineyards A-REIT
http://www.challenger.com.au/listed/cwt/cwt.asp

Charter Hall Group—commercial real estate properties and funds
http://www.charterhall.com.au/

Cheviot Kirribilly Vineyard Property Group—Australian vineyards
http://www.cheviotkirribilly.com.au/

Cromwell Corporation Limited—diversified A-REIT with funds management
http://www.cromwell.com.au/home/

Commonwealth Property—office buildings in Australia
http://www.cfsgam.com.au/cpa/HomeCPA.aspx

Coonawarra Australia—Australian vineyard
http://www.coonawarravineyard.com.au/

REITs Around the World

Compass Hotel Group—hotels and taverns
http://www.compasshotel.com.au/

DEXUS Property Group—large owner of commercial properties worldwide
http://www.dexus.com/

Galileo Japan Trust—Tokyo area office buildings
http://www.galileofunds.com.au/Japan/index.html

GEO Property Group Limited—residential property development
http://www.geopg.com.au/index.asp

Goodman Group—worldwide business and industrial properties
http://www.goodman.com/

GPT Group—large diversified A-REIT
http://www.gpt.com.au/

Growthpoint Properties Australia—commercial properties in Australia
http://www.growthpoint.co.za/GrowthpointOZ.aspx

Hedley Leisure and Gaming Property Fund—freehold pub market
http://www.hlg.com.au/

ING Real Estate Entertainment Fund—entertainment and leisure A-REIT
http://www.ingrealestate.com/au_en/investing/listed_real_estate_investment_trusts/ingre_entertainment_fund/

ING Real Estate Healthcare Fund—healthcare sector properties
http://www.ingrealestate.com/au_en/investing/listed_real_estate_investment_trusts/ingre_health_care_fund/index.jsp

ING Industrial Fund—over 500 business parks and industrial properties
http://www.ingrealestate.com/au_en/investing/listed_real_estate_investment_trusts/ing_industrial_fund

ING Office Fund—office buildings worldwide
http://www.ingrealestate.com/au_en/investing/listed_real_estate_investment_trusts/ing_office_fund/

ING Real Estate Community Living—housing for students and senior citizens http://www.ingrealestate.com/au_en/investing/listed_real_estate_investment_trusts/ingre_community_living_group/

Living and Lesiure Australia Group—skiing resorts and other leisure properties
http://www.livingandleisure.com.au/

MacarthurCook Property Securities Fund—diversified commercial properties in Australia
http://www.macarthurcook.com.au/MCK/EN/Investments_Funds/Investment.aspx?id=2

MacarthurCook Industrial Property Fund—Australian industries properties
http://www.macarthurcook.com.au/MCK/EN/Investments_Funds/Investment.aspx?Id=11&categoryId=3

Macquarie Countrywide—supermarket anchored shopping centers
http://www.macquarie.com.au/au/property/mcw/index.html

Macquarie DDR—shopping centers in the United States
http://www.macquarie.com.au/au/property/mdt/index.html

Macquarie Office Trust—high grade office buildings
http://www.macquarie.com.au/au/property/mof/index.html

Mariner American Property Income Trust—owns commercial real estate in the United States
http://www.marinerfunds.com.au/funds/property-funds/mariner-american-property-income-trust

Mirvac Group—diversified commercial properties
http://www.mirvac.com/home

Mirvac Industrial Trust—greater Chicago area industrial properties
http://www.mirvac.com/investmentmanagement/mix/home

Mirvac Real Estate Investment Trust—diversified properties including Travelodges
http://www.mirvac.com/home

Multiplex Acumen Prime Property Fund—Sydney and Melbourne offices
http://www.brookfieldmultiplexcapital.com/investment-funds/multiplex-prime-property-fund/

Multiplex Acumen Property Fund—invests in unlisted property funds
http://www.brookfieldmultiplexcapital.com/investment-funds/multiplex-acumen-property-fund/

REITs Around the World

Prime Retirement and Aged Care Property Trust—retirement villages and nursing homes in Australia
http://www.primetrust.com.au/

Rabinov Property Trust—named after Ezriel Rabinowicz
http://www.rabinov.com.au/

RNY Property Trust—New York City office buildings
http://www.rnypt.com.au/Web/RECKWebContent.aspx

Rubicon America Trust—diversified commercial real estate properties across the United States
http://www.rubiconamerica.com.au/

Rubicon Europe Trust Group—diversified commercial properties in Germany, Belgium and The Netherlands
http://www.rubiconeurope.com.au/default.asp

Rubicon Japan Trust—owns properties in Japan
http://www.rubiconjapan.com.au/

Stockland—in top 50 of ASX stocks
http://www.stockland.com.au/

Thakral Holdings Group—commercial and hotel properties
http://www.thakral.com.au/

Timbercorp Primary Infrastructure—agribusiness infrastructure
http://www.tpif.com.au/

Tishman Speyer Office Fund—office buildings in major US markets
http://www.tishmanspeyer.com.au/irm/content/home.html

Trafalgar Corporate—diversified, stapled real estate properties
http://www.trafalgarcorporate.com/index.htm

Trinity Limited—commercial properties and funds management
http://www.trinity.com.au/

Valad Property Group—commercial properties in Australia, New Zealand and United States
http://www.valad.com.au/

Westfield Group—major worldwide shopping centers company
http://westfield.com/corporate/

Westfield Retail Trust—spin off of shopping centers in Australia
http://www.westfieldretailtrust.com/

Westpac Office Trust—offices in Australia and New Zealand
https://www.westpacfunds.com.au/officetrust.asp

Chapter Forty-Three

Real Estate Investment Trusts in New Zealand

In contrast with every other country with Real Estate Investment Trusts, New Zealand has not created legal REITs with one specific law. Therefore, there technically are no New Zealand Real Estate Investment Trusts. However, some companies use other existing business structures to achieve the same end. That is, creation of a "flow through" entity engaged in the business of real estate without the obligation to pay corporate income taxes.

This has been possible since either 1969 or 1971. I've seen both dates given.

Unit Trusts as Real Estate Investment Trusts in New Zealand

Unit trusts can invest in real estate. These are regulated by the trust deed. Investment by investors outside New Zealand may require consent by the Overseas Investment Office. Unit trusts are generally taxed as companies at the prevailing corporate tax rate, whether they're listed or unlisted.

Investing in real estate does not qualify unit trusts for any special tax considerations.

For individual tax purposes, the distributions of unit trusts are treated the same as dividends from corporations. Under some circumstances, however, some of the amounts distributed are considered as returns of unit capital or on buybacks of units, and therefore may be excluded from treatment as dividends, and therefore are not taxable in New Zealand.

A non-resident withholding tax (NRWT) of 30% is applied to distributions to unit owners outside New Zealand.

Richard Stooker

Portfolio Investment Entities - PIEs as New Zealand REITs

As of October 1, 2007 businesses may choose to be Portfolio Investment Entities (PIE). PIE characteristics include:

Flow-through (income not taxed at this level)

Broad passive investment categories

Various eligibility criteria

May include listed or unlisted unit trusts, group investment funds, superannuation (similar to US IRAs) funds or companies may qualify

There are restrictions on leasing land from a person associated with the PIE (an obvious attempt to prevent conflicts of interest.)

90% of portfolio must be passive, and other restrictions apply

For PIEs listed on the New Zealand Stock Exchange, distributions are taxable to the extent they have New Zealand imputation credits attached.

Foreign owners of PIE shares are also subject to the 30% non-resident withholding tax.

Limited Partnerships as New Zealand Real Estate Investment Trusts

As of May 2, 2008 companies may choose Limited Partnerships (LP). LP characteristics include:

They must have at least one general partner and limited partner.

The limited partner's liability is limited to their investment in the partnership

Listed LPs and some foreign LPs are treated as companies, therefore with no flow-through.

Since this site is to help ordinary investors, I write about only listed securities. Therefore, private limited partnerships in New Zealand that invest in real estate are useless for us.

From what I've learned, REITs in New Zealand have less short term debt, did not invest in mortgage-backed securities, use less leverage (or gearing) and do not invest in real estate properties outside New Zealand. Unlike their close neighbors in Australia, they do not use stapled securities, but rely on their property investments. They generally focus on commercial

156

real property.

New Zealand REITs Include:

1. AMP Property Trust

2. Tower Property Trust, Property for Industry, Capital Properties

3. Mint Australia New Zealand Real Estate Investment Trust

4. AMP NZ Office Trust

5. ING Property Trust

6. The National Property Trust

7. Century City Ltd

8. DNZ Property Group

9. Epsilon International Property Group (EIPG)
http://www.eipg.co.nz/

10. Franklin Rural Management Ltd

11. ING Medical Properties Trust

12. Property for Industry Ltd

13. Redwood Group Ltd
http://www.redwoodgroup.co.nz/

14. Rural Equities Ltd
http://www.ruralequities.co.nz/

15. Stepladder (formerly Home Investments Ltd)
http://www.stepladder.co.nz/content/

16. Todd Property Group Limited

17. MGPSA New Zealand REIT (AMEPRTNZ:IND)

18. Kermadec Property Fund Ltd (KPF:NZ - diversified portfolio
http://www.kermadecproperty.co.nz/

19. Kingston Properties Ltd (KPREIT:JA

20. Kiwi Income Property Trust (KIP:NZ)—14 properties in New Zealand
http://www.kipt.co.nz/

21. Argosy Property Trust—one of the largest REITs in New Zealand
http://www.argosy.co.nz/

Chapter Forty-Four

How to Invest in REITS Around the World

OK, it's always fun to make a trip. We've gone around the world and now we're back home (wherever home is for you).

Do we retrace our steps and, like Jim Rogers (author of Investment Biker and Adventure Capitalist - both highly recommended) open up local brokerage accounts and buy shares of all the REITs we visited?

Sure, if - like Rogers - you're already so overwhelmingly rich from having run a hedge fund with George Soros you can afford to indulge yourself and take risks with what was no doubt a tiny percentage of his total fortune. (And know you can get well paid to write a book about your trip as well.)

Many of the countries I just covered have only a few REITs. Some place many restrictions on how they can make money. Some of the REITs are brand new. Many are required to pay dividends only once a year—and long after the close of the period. Most REITs are required to pay the same 90% US REITs are, but others don't have to pay that much.

Some REITs are in countries where the commercial real estate market is very unstable and not transparent. In some places it's common for sales to not be recorded, because neither party wants to pay the required taxes. Many such countries have passed REIT laws in hopes of helping their local markets become more mature and transparent.

Some of these countries have trouble maintaining law and order against ordinary criminals. They probably don't have the resources to go after "white collar" fraud.

Pioneering investors who buy up companies in such countries may well make a lot of money in the long run—I believe the world's wealth is on the increase and transparency will increase—but I am interested in Real Estate Investment Trusts as an income investment, not a long-term possible capital gain. I advocate receiving an ROI right away, not years in the future.

Even in Europe, you can't count on dividends being paid on a regular quarterly schedule as is the custom in the US.

Yet I'm not saying to stick with only US REITs if you live in the US. There are many great US REIT companies—far more than most of us can afford to buy up—but there are also great opportunities outside the US that should not be ignored.

Buying Shares of Any One REIT is Too Risky

However, I don't recommend you buy any one company. Any one company can be hit with a disaster and go out of business even while the rest of the REIT industry is booming.

Therefore, you should buy REIT indexes, and the best way to do that is through Exchange Traded Funds (ETF).

I don't have room here to explain Exchange Traded Funds. I do that in my book Income Investing Secrets, and also explain why they're so much better than mutual funds.

I'll just say an ETF is an investment which is basically a basket or pool of securities similar to a mutual fund. But you can buy and sell ETF shares through your broker just as though they were ordinary shares of stock. They go up and down in price depending on the market prices of the basket of securities. Unlike mutual funds, you always know what you own, because it's a public index. You can always look it up.

As long as you own shares of an ETF, you get paid dividends from the securities they hold. That amount depends on how much—and when – the money is paid out.

If necessary, you can tell your broker to sell the 100 ETF shares and it'll be done right away just like shares of stocks.

It's a lot easier than a mutual fund. And, because you don't have a manager actively trying to "beat" the European REIT market, the EFT company doesn't send out statements or staff 800 customer service lines, it's a lot cheaper.

REIT ETFs—U.S. Only

Some Exchange Traded Funds track only REITs in specialized sections of the real estate markets, such as residential or commercial or retail REITs. For simplicity, and for greater diversification, I'm leaving these out. I'm including only those ETFs that track a broad cross-section of the total US REIT marketplace. I'm also not including any that are leveraged - they're too risky.)

Also, these cover equity REITs only. Mortgage REITs are much more risky. They make money not from operating real estate, but loaning out money.

1. Vanguard REIT ETF: VNQ

The Vanguard REIT ETF tracks the performance of the MSCI® US REIT Index. Expense ratio 0.12%.

2. The iShares FTSE NAREIT Real Estate 50 Index Fund: FTY

Tracks the performance of the FTSE NAREIT Real Estate 50 Index. Expense ratio 0.48%.

3. SPDR Dow Jones REIT ETF: RWR

Tracks the Dow Jones U.S. Select REIT Index. Expense ratio 0.26%.

4. iShares Cohen & Steers Realty Majors Index Fund: ICF

The iShares Cohen & Steers Realty Majors Index Fund tracks the performance of the Cohen & Steers Realty Majors Index. Expense ratio is 0.35%.

5. iShares Dow Jones U.S. Real Estate Index Fund: IYR

This ETF tracks the performance of the Dow Jones U.S. Real Estate Index. Expense ratio 0.47%.

6. Guggenheim Wilshire U.S. Real Estate Investment Trust ETF WREI

Tracks the Wilshire US Real Estate Investment Trust Index(SM). Expense ratio is 0.32%.

7. First Trust S&P REIT Idx FRI

Tracks the S&P United States REIT Index. Expense ratio is 0.50%.

8. PowerShares Active U.S. Real Estate (PSR)

Tracks the FTSE NAREIT Equity REITs Index by at least 80%. Expense ratio is 0.80%.

There's no point in buying more than one of these, as all of them will give you results that roughly correspond to the overall U.S. REIT market.

My personal vote is for VNQ, because Vanguard keeps the expense ratios of their funds as low as possible.

REIT ETFs—Outside U.S.

I'm including only those REITs that are open to including REITs from any country except the United States. Country-specific REITs are too risky.

1. SPDR Dow Jones International Real Estate ETF: RWX

This ETF tracks the Dow Jones Global ex-U.S. Select Real Estate Securities Index. Expense ratio is 0.59%.

Top Holdings:

1. Unibail-Rodamco Se
2. Westfield Group
3. Brookfield Asset Mgmt Inc
4. Mitsui Fudosan Co
5. Land Securities Gp
6. Hang Lung Prop
7. Hongkong Land Holdings
8. British Land Co
9. Westfield Retail
10. Link R/EstInvest

2. S&P Developed ex-U.S. Property Index Fund: WPS

Tracks the S&P/ Developed ex-U.S Property Index. Expense ratio is 0.48%.

Top Holdings:

1. Mitsubishi Estate Co Ltd
2. Sun Hing Kai Properties
3. Unibail-Rodamco SE
4. Westfield Group
5. Cheung Kong Holdings Ltd
6. Mitsui Fudosan Co Ltd
7. Sumitomo Realty & Development
8. Land Securities Group PLC

9. Link REIT
10. Daito Trust Construct Co Ltd

3. WisdomTree International Real Estate Fund: DRW

Tracks the WisdomTree International Real Estate Index. Expense ratio is 0.58%.

Top Holdings

1. Westfielddg Stapled
2. Gecina
3. Unibail-Rodamco
5. Klepierre
6. British Land Co
7. GPT Stapled

4. iShares FTSE EPRA/NAREIT Global Real Estate ex-U.S. Index ETF IFGL

Tracks the FTSE EPRA/NAREIT Developed Real Estate ex-U.S. Index. Expense ratio is 0.48%.

Top Holdings:

1. Sun Hung Kai Properties
2. Unibail-Rodamco SE
3. Westfield Group
4. Mitsubishi Estate Co Ltd
5. Mitsui Fudosan Co Ltd
6. Sumitomo Realty & Development
7. Hongkong Land Holdings
8. Land Securities Group PLC
9. Westfield Retail
10. Link REIT

These ETFs are not 100% REITs. Some of their holdings are listed real estate companies that don't meet REIT requirements.

Selecting which one of these to buy is a tough call. International REIT ETFs can vary a lot in performance by holding different percentages of ETFs in different parts of the world.

I'd eliminate #2 and #3 right away because their expense ratios are substantially higher. The other two are tied at 0.48%.

Both #1 and #4 hold shares in many Asian REITs, with some of the larger European ones.

But #4 tracks an index created by FTSE (a European indexing company) in conjunction with both NAREIT and EPRA, two of the world's major REIT professional organizations.

If anybody should be expert at the world's REITs, it's those two groups.

Therefore, my recommendation is to buy iShares FTSE EPRA/NAREIT Global Real Estate ex-U.S. Index ETF IFGL.

Canada Only

1. **iShares CDN REIT Index Fund (XRE)**

Expense ratio is 0.55%. It's listed on the Toronto Stock Exchange.

Top Holdings:

1. Riocan REIT
2. H&R REIT
3. Calloway REIT
4. Canadian REIT
5. Dundee REIT
6. Boardwalk
7. Primaris
8. Canadian Apartment Properties REIT
9. Allied Properties
10. Cominar

For More Info:

For more information on US REITs, grab the latest edition of Ralph L. Block's book Investing in REITs: Real Estate Investment Trusts:

http://www.amazon.com/Investing-REITs-Estate-Investment-Bloomberg/dp/1118004450

For more information on all REITs, especially the individual companies, go to my website:

http://www.incomeinvesthome.com/growth/reit/

http://www.incomeinvestingsecrets.com/

www.ingramcontent.com/pod-product-compliance
Lightning Source LLC
Chambersburg PA
CBHW081258170526
45165CB00011B/3344